ISTRIBUTED GENERATION IN LIBERALISED ELECTRICITY MARKETS

INTERNATIONAL ENERGY AGENCY

INTERNATIONAL ENERGY AGENCY
9, rue de la Fédération,
75739 Paris, cedex 15, France

ORGANISATION FOR ECONOMIC CO-OPERATION AND DEVELOPMENT

The International Energy Agency (IEA) is an autonomous body which was established in November 1974 within the framework of the Organisation for Economic Co-operation and Development (OECD) to implement an international energy programme.

It carries out a comprehensive programme of energy co-operation among twenty-six* of the OECD's thirty Member countries. The basic aims of the IEA are:

- to maintain and improve systems for coping with oil supply disruptions;

- to promote rational energy policies in a global context through co-operative relations with non-member countries, industry and international organisations;

- to operate a permanent information system on the international oil market;

- to improve the world's energy supply and demand structure by developing alternative energy sources and increasing the efficiency of energy use;

- to assist in the integration of environmental and energy policies.

IEA Member countries: Australia, Austria, Belgium, Canada, the Czech Republic, Denmark, Finland, France, Germany, Greece, Hungary, Ireland, Italy, Japan, the Republic of Korea, Luxembourg, the Netherlands, New Zealand, Norway, Portugal, Spain, Sweden, Switzerland, Turkey, the United Kingdom, the United States. The European Commission also takes part in the work of the IEA.

Pursuant to Article 1 of the Convention signed in Paris on 14th December 1960, and which came into force on 30th September 1961, the Organisation for Economic Co-operation and Development (OECD) shall promote policies designed:

- to achieve the highest sustainable economic growth and employment and a rising standard of living in Member countries, while maintaining financial stability, and thus to contribute to the development of the world economy;

- to contribute to sound economic expansion in Member as well as non-member countries in the process of economic development; and

- to contribute to the expansion of world trade on a multilateral, non-discriminatory basis in accordance with international obligations.

The original Member countries of the OECD are Austria, Belgium, Canada, Denmark, France, Germany, Greece, Iceland, Ireland, Italy, Luxembourg, the Netherlands, Norway, Portugal, Spain, Sweden, Switzerland, Turkey, the United Kingdom and the United States. The following countries became Members subsequently through accession at the dates indicated hereafter: Japan (28th April 1964), Finland (28th January 1969), Australia (7th June 1971), New Zealand (29th May 1973), Mexico (18th May 1994), the Czech Republic (21st December 1995), Hungary (7th May 1996), Poland (22nd November 1996), the Republic of Korea (12th December 1996) and Slovakia (28th September 2000). The Commission of the European Communities takes part in the work of the OECD (Article 13 of the OECD Convention).

FOREWORD

Early electric power systems consisted of small generation plants located near consumers. Although most power today is produced in large central generation plants, small-scale "distributed" generation is enjoying a renaissance. Power consumers are using distributed generation technologies to ensure very high electrical reliability, to provide capacity in emergencies and, in some cases, to displace costly electricity from the grid. Network owners are using distributed generation to defer investments in network expansion.

This book provides a guide to energy policy makers on this growing phenomenon. It surveys the status of distributed generation in selected OECD countries. It looks at the economics of distributed generation versus central generation. It identifies key regulatory barriers. It discusses the environmental and energy security implications of these technologies.

This book also looks ahead to a future in which a substantial share of electricity is produced by distributed generation. Such a future would require a fundamental redesign of the electricity system. While our analysis finds that distributed generation is not yet ready to replace existing systems, there are changes to regulations and market rules which could ensure that it finds its proper place.

The principal author of this report is Peter Fraser. Shin Morita provided substantial assistance on Japan.

Robert Priddle
Executive Director

TABLE OF CONTENTS

LIST OF TABLES

LIST OF FIGURES

EXECUTIVE SUMMARY

Most of the electricity produced in the OECD is generated in large generating stations. These stations produce and transmit electricity through high-voltage transmission systems then, at reduced voltage, transmit it through local distribution systems to consumers. Some electricity is produced by distributed-generation (DG) plants. In contrast with large generating stations, they produce power on a customer's site or at a local distribution utility, and supply power directly to the local distribution network. DG technologies include engines, small turbines, fuel cells, and photovoltaic systems.

Although they represent a small share of the electricity market, distributed-generation technologies already play a key role: for applications in which reliability is crucial, as a source of emergency capacity, and as an alternative to expansion of a local network. In some markets, they are actually displacing more costly grid electricity. Worldwide, more DG capacity was ordered in 2000 than for new nuclear power. Government policies favouring combined heat and power (CHP) generation, and renewable energy and technological development should assure growth of distributed generation. This kind of generation has the potential to alter fundamentally the structure and organisation of our electric power system. Yet market conditions in some countries pose serious challenges to some generators, particularly those producing combined heat and power.

This book provides a guide to this growing phenomenon by:

■ surveying the current situation and market status of distributed generation in selected OECD countries, including the impact of current energy policies;

■ examining the economic, environmental, and energy-security implications of wider deployment of various DG technologies as well as the consequences for electricity transmission and distribution; and

■ making general recommendations for accommodating distributed generation into liberalised electricity markets.

Distributed-generation Technologies

Diesel and gas reciprocating engines and gas turbines are well-established technologies. Industrial-sized engines and turbines can achieve fuel efficiencies in excess of 40% and are low in cost per kilowatt. These big engines and turbines accounted for most new DG capacity installed in the year 2000, of approximately 20 GW or 10% of total new electricity capacity. While nearly half of the capacity was ordered for standby use, the demand for units for continuous or peaking use has been increasing.

Other DG technologies have yet to make a large commercial impact. Microturbines are a new technology. They have lower emissions than engines, but their capital cost is higher. Their fuel economy is similar to that of natural gas engines. Fuel cells are the object of much research and development, primarily for transportation applications. They have been deployed for power generation in a limited way, but their capital costs will need to drop sharply to be competitive. The cost of photovoltaic systems, while still high, is expected to go on falling over the next decade.

Economics of Distributed Generation

Distributed generation has some economic advantages over power from the grid, particularly for on-site power production:

■ On-site production avoids transmission and distribution costs, which otherwise amount to about 30% of the cost of delivered electricity.

■ Onsite power production by fossil fuels generates waste heat that can be used by the customer.

■ Distributed generation may also be better positioned to use inexpensive fuels such as landfill gas.

On the other hand, DG has higher unit capital costs per kilowatt than a large plant. It has lower fuel economy, unless used in CHP mode, and uses a more limited selection of fuels. For photovoltaic systems, operating costs are very low but high capital costs make it uncompetitive.

The relative price of retail electricity compared with fuel costs is critical to the competitiveness of any distributed-generation option. This ratio varies greatly from country to country. In Japan, for example, where electricity and natural gas prices are high, DG is attractive only for oil-fired generation. In other countries, where gas is inexpensive compared with electricity, distributed generation with gas can become economically attractive.

Conventional economic assessments of generating options tend to understate the value of the flexibility of a distributed generation plant to its owner. Many DG technologies can be very flexible in their operation, size, and expandability. A distributed generation plant can operate during periods of high electricity prices (peak periods) and then switch off during periods of low prices. The ease of installation of DG allows capacity to be expanded readily to take advantage of anticipated high prices. Some DG assets are portable. They can literally "follow the market". New analytical techniques, such as "real option valuation", can quantify the economic value of flexibility.

In addition to this technological flexibility, a distributed generator may add value to some power systems by delaying the need to upgrade a congested transmission or distribution network, by reducing distribution losses, and by providing support or ancillary services to the local distribution network.

CHP is economically attractive for distributed generation because of its higher fuel efficiency and low incremental capital costs for heat-recovery equipment. The size of the CHP system matters: the most economical match the heat load. Economies of scale also matter. More than 80% of CHP capacity is in large industrial applications, mostly in four industries: paper, chemicals, petroleum refining, and food processing. Even so, much of the CHP capacity in the OECD has been developed as a consequence of supportive government policies. Such policies have also encouraged systems to produce power for export to the grid.

CHP for domestic use, called "micro-CHP", is attracting much interest, particularly where it uses external combustion engines and in some cases fuel cells. Despite the potential for a short payback period, high capital costs for the domestic consumer are a barrier to the penetration of these two technologies.

The provision of reliable power represents the most important market niche for DG. Emergency diesel generating capacity in buildings is generally not built to export power to the grid. If it could be exported, it would represent several percent of total peak demand for electricity. The existence of this neglected source of potential grid power is gaining increased attention, particularly in the United States, where demand growth has led to tighter capacity margins. In the summer of 2001, system operators in New Mexico and Oregon arranged for the use of existing standby generators to supply additional power to the grid under emergency conditions.

In addition to improving the reliability of grid electricity, DG can serve growing consumer demand for higher quality electricity. Electricity consumers who require higher electric reliability than the grid can normally provide, i.e. in continuous manufacturing processes or Internet services, are looking to distributed generation to assure a continuous supply of power. Two DG technologies are potentially superior in this regard:

■ fuel cells, and

■ backup systems comprising gas engines combined with uninterrupted power supplies (such as flywheels), which recently have been commercialised.

While this kind of capacity will contribute only a very small part of overall electricity production, it is likely to become an increasingly important source of peak supply and a bigger factor in electricity-supply security.

DG can also have economic applications to meet off-grid needs, such as in communities remote from the main grid. Photovoltaic systems combined with battery storage, for example, can be the most economical method of powering remote lighting, telephone, and other low capacity applications.

Distributed Generation in Japan, the US, the Netherlands, and the UK

The status of distributed generation differs in each OECD country. While economics is certainly a fundamental factor, government policy also affects the role of distributed generation. This report examines these and other influences on the development of distributed generation in Japan, the US, the Netherlands, and the UK.

Distributed generation is a viable option in Japan because of high prices and limited market opening for electricity. There are three common types of DG in the country: oil-fired generation, designed principally to meet peak demand; oil-fired CHP using diesel engines and steam turbines; and gas-fired CHP with engines, gas or steam turbines. The high retail price of natural gas in Japan makes gas-fired distributed generation without CHP uneconomical. Gas-fired CHP is only marginally economical but is the only DG option in Tokyo, Yokohama, and Osaka, due to tight environmental regulations. A survey by the Japan Engine Generator Association (NEGA) estimates that from 1997 to 2000, installation of distributed generation, excluding emergency power, grew by 2 418 MW, or about 11% of the amount installed by the utilities during the period. Distributed generation is recognised as a business opportunity for the utilities. Eight of the ten electric utilities in Japan have established subsidiaries to offer DG services.

Japan has removed several regulatory barriers to encourage the development of distributed generation and, in particular, cogeneration systems. These actions include adjustments to fire regulations and on-site staffing requirements. However, some regulatory barriers still remain. Selling excess distributed generation to another electricity customer generally is not allowed. The costs of electrical protection equipment can be substantial: about 10% of the total cost of the facility or more.

Distributed generation in the US is limited by low electricity prices and affected by the widely varied pace of electricity-market liberalisation in the 50 states. CHP accounts for 50.4 GW, or about 6% of total US electrical generating capacity, nearly all in large industrial plants. Emergency power generators in buildings have been identified as a potential source of emergency capacity for the grid. A detailed survey of standby generators in California by the California Energy Commission found 3.2 GW of such capacity, equivalent to more than 6% of peak electricity demand in the state[1].

Aside from economic competitiveness, there are several challenges to the growth of distributed generation in the US. Obtaining a permit for a site is difficult and expensive on a per-kilowatt basis. The lack of a national standard for interconnection further increases transaction costs, even though such a standard is now under development. Incomplete regulatory reform has left distribution utilities competing with distributed generation. Environmental standards have been toughened in some states, with the same standard applied regardless of the size of the generator. This approach effectively limits fossil-fired DG in these states.

The Netherlands has an advanced liberalised market where distributed generation is well-established, principally because government policies have supported CHP and renewable energy sources. But the general policy thrust in Holland is to avoid using favourable grid policies or tariffs to subsidise the development of these technologies, and to rely instead on other methods. The substantial Dutch experience with DG has had some important advantages. Unlike the situation in the US, interconnection rules in the Netherlands are standardised. Market rules were adjusted soon after their introduction so that CHP producers could more accurately predict how much electricity to

---

1. CEC, 2001.

supply to the grid. Power parks have been established where the main producer is the only customer with a direct connection to the grid. But CHP producers still faced difficulties because of rising gas prices and falling electricity prices. To help them cope, the Dutch government has increased direct subsidies to producers and has encouraged distribution companies to ensure that the network value of distributed generation is appropriately reflected in tariffs.

The United Kingdom, which also has an advanced liberalised market, has policies that favour development of CHP and renewables as well. The government has set targets for increasing the contributions of renewables, from around 2% in 2000 to 10% by 2010, and CHP, from 4.6 GW to 10 GW by 2010. The government has also identified the development of embedded generation as an important way to increase competition among electricity producers.

New electricity trading rules, known as the New Electricity Trading Arrangements (NETA), nonetheless have been disadvantageous to small embedded generators. The rules require that all generators predict their output at least 3.5 hours in advance of actual production; they face penalties if they produce less than forecast but receive only modest remuneration for supplying more. So far NETA has resulted in a drop in electricity prices and a decline in power produced for the grid by embedded generators.

In anticipation of these problems, the UK government commissioned an Embedded Generation Working Group to examine the role of DG in the liberalised market. The group's report, issued in January 2001, identified a number of practical measures to ensure DG is integrated into the power system in an economically efficient way. The government and the regulator (Ofgem) have both acted on the report's recommendations by:

■ proposing new principles for setting tariffs and simpler rules for grid connection;

■ requiring distributors to provide additional information on the value of distributed generation at different points in their grid; and

■ establishing a Distributed Generation Co-ordinating Group to follow up on the Working Group's recommendations.

Policy Issues

Policy issues affecting distributed generation can be grouped under the three Es of energy policy: economic efficiency, environmental protection, and energy security. Under the heading of economic efficiency, issues include:

- market access, i.e. the connection of distributed generation to distribution grids and to distribution networks;
- pricing, i.e. incorporating the benefits and costs of distributed power in distribution-network tariffs; and
- market conditions.

In the area of environment, the report considers the emissions performance of different DG technologies and whether environmental regulations could limit the deployment of DG. As for energy security, the report examines the implications of distributed generation for the diversification of fuels and on the reliability of the electricity network.

■ Economic Efficiency

Connecting distributed generation to the distribution grid can impair the performance and reliability of the local grid, which is normally designed to deliver power to end users. Connection thus creates a technical problem, particularly without standard rules.

Costs incurred by the local grid operator to connect DG can be substantial, especially if the distribution system must be reinforced. These costs need to be recovered from either the DG producer or power consumers. The principle of economic efficiency suggests that the producer should pay all of the costs of upgrading the distribution system. However, large central generators, which compete with DG producers, do not have to pay for transmission-system upgrades. Under these circumstances, the only fair solution is for DG plant owners to pay direct connection costs and for all users to pay the remainder in the form of operating charges.

In Western Europe, market liberalisation has negatively affected distributed generation, particularly on CHP, mainly because natural gas prices have risen as electricity prices have fallen. In response, governments in some countries have increased their financial support to CHP producers. Yet market liberalisation is exposing *all* power producers to the vagaries of the marketplace. DG producers, like other producers, have to respond. In the long run, the current challenges by themselves may encourage more efficient and less expensive development of DG.

Liberalisation of the electricity market, in fact, is not broad enough. Prices are not sensitive to location, a key value of distributed generation. For example, electricity distribution losses vary from less than 1% to 20% or more depending on the voltage and the location of the consumer. Location also plays a role in the value of distributed generation in deferring expansion of transmission infrastructure, providing ancillary services or relieving distribution congestion. While retail liberalisation may be a necessary condition for the DG development, it is not sufficient to ensure nondiscriminatory access. Utilities that own generating capacity or supply customers directly will continue to have an incentive to discriminate against DG. To avoid such discrimination, regulatory vigilance will be needed.

In certain markets where they can avoid charges on transmission, distributed generators may have an advantage over central generation. Elsewhere, in wholesale markets that are designed with large central generation in mind, smaller distributed generators may be at a disadvantage because of the additional costs and complexities of dealing with the market. Difficulties in the NETA market in the UK and in the new Dutch market suggest that further market measures are needed to make the system fair to smaller generators.

Pricing reforms that accompany market liberalisation can benefit distributed generation. These reforms will raise the price of electricity during peak periods and thus make distributed generation more economical. The application of time-of-use rates in Japan is credited with the installation of cogeneration systems that operate only during peak hours.

■ Environmental Protection

Distributed generation embraces a wide range of technologies with a wide range of emissions. For fossil-fired distributed technologies, there are two key areas of concern: NO_x emissions on local/regional air quality and greenhouse-gas emissions on climate change.

Emissions per kilowatt-hour of NO_x from distributed generation (except by diesel generators) tend to be lower than those from a coal-fired power plant or a utility system using a large proportion of coal. At the same time, the emissions rate from existing distributed generation (except by fuel cells and PV) are higher than the "best available" central generation: a combined-cycle gas turbine with advanced emissions control. This disadvantage puts a serious limitation on distributed generation in areas where NO_x emissions are rigorously controlled, even when DG could reduce overall emissions sharply.

The case of carbon-dioxide emissions is similar. Emissions rates for distributed generation are generally lower than those for coal plants, but not as low as those for new combined cycles – except for DG used in CHP mode. Measures can be designed that encourage distributed generators to reduce emissions. The use of economic instruments like carbon-emissions trading, for example, would give DG operators an incentive to design and operate their facilities in ways that minimise emissions of greenhouse gases.

■ Energy Security

The implications of distributed generation for energy security take two forms:

■ on the diversification of primary energy supplies; and
■ on the reliability of electricity supply.

The effect on primary fuels depends on the underlying technology. Photovoltaic systems help diversify supply away from fossil fuels. Most of the other technologies rely directly or indirectly on natural gas. Since much of the new investment in DG is for natural gas, the effect on fuel diversity in the power system is limited. The exception is CHP, as its higher fuel efficiency (compared with separate heat and power facilities) means lower fuel consumption and thus enhanced energy security.

The reliability of electric power systems can be enhanced by distributed generation. The availability of standby generators in the US electricity market in the summer of 2001 helped reduce the risk of blackouts. Better integration of standby resources into the system would further enhance security of supply. Furthermore, the use of distributed generators at selected locations helps distributors overcome local bottlenecks. Increasing distributed generation could reduce the demand for transmission, thereby increasing margins on transmission lines. Ultimately, a power system based on a large number of reliable small generators can operate with the same reliability and a lower capacity margin than a system of equally reliable large generators.

The main drawback of distributed generation for energy security would be a weakening of the network's ability to supply primary reserve power if DG cannot respond to load changes. This would be the case if most DG capacity is nondispatchable because of natural variability (wind and photovoltaic systems) or operating variability (CHP where power output is tied to heat demand). The operators of the Nordel system have identified the expansion of wind and CHP as a reliability concern and are studying how best to address it. They have suggested that the operational control of the network may need to be decentralised by creating a system operator for each Nordel subarea.

Future of Distributed Generation in Electricity Networks

The wide range of potential applications and favourable government policies for CHP and for renewables should ensure greater market share for distributed generation over the next decade. But further research and development is needed to reduce costs and improve environmental performance. Substantial R&D money is already being directed to fuel cells and photovoltaic systems. Investments are also needed to reduce the capital costs and improve the efficiency of microturbines. Improvements in the environmental performance of engines and small turbines also will be needed, to ensure that their NO_x emissions do not preclude deployment. Further developments in combining DG with cooling or with uninterrupted-power supply technologies would enhance its attractiveness.

Despite the limited penetration of distributed power in today's markets, the future will probably see an evolution to a much more decentralised power system. Such a system could have advantages with respect to security and reliability of supply. It could emerge from the present system in three stages:

■ accommodation of distributed generation in the current system;

■ the creation of decentralised network system that works in tandem with a centralised generation system; and

■ a dispersed system where most power is generated by decentralised stations and a limited amount by central generation.

There are a few signs that electricity networks are beginning this evolution. For example, new technologies are already being used to control output from distributed generation at several sites to respond to market conditions, creating a kind of "virtual utility". The operation of a network with a large number of virtual utilities will require much greater real-time information flow than is now the case. For the present, however, there is a need to redesign distribution systems simply to accommodate DG.

INTRODUCTION

Electric power systems in OECD countries are organised to supply electricity mainly through the co-ordinated operation of large generating stations that produce and transmit electricity through high-voltage transmission systems then, at reduced voltage, send the power through local distribution systems to consumers. Some electricity is produced by distributed generation (DG) plants. They differ from the large generating stations in producing power on a customer's site where some or all is consumed and in sending any surplus power directly to the local distribution network. Distributed generation can also be used by a distributor to deliver additional power to the local distribution network. Figure I illustrates where DG and energy-storage technologies fit into an electricity network.

What is Distributed Generation?

Many terms have emerged to describe power that comes elsewhere than from large generating units exporting electricity into a high voltage network. Because there are no universally accepted terms, this report uses the following ones:

Distributed generation *is generating plant serving a customer on-site or providing support to a distribution network, connected to the grid at distribution-level voltages. The technologies generally include engines, small (and micro) turbines, fuel cells, and photovoltaic systems. It generally excludes wind power, since that is mostly produced on wind farms rather than for on-site power requirements.*

Dispersed generation *is distributed generation plus wind power and other generation, either connected to a distribution network or completely independent of the grid.*

Distributed power is distributed generation plus energy-storage technologies such as flywheels, large regenerative fuel cells, or compressed air storage.

Distributed energy resources refer to distributed generation plus demand-side measures.

Decentralised power refers to a system of distributed-energy resources connected to a distribution network.

The importance of distributed generation varies by country. In the Netherlands, about half of total electricity generation is from large CHP plants supplying electricity to local distribution networks. In many other countries, however, most DG is used on-site; little or no power is made available to the local network. Most DG capacity in the OECD is provided by diesel engines for emergency power, not power production.

Distributed generation is attracting increasing interest and policy attention. There are five major factors behind this trend: electricity market liberalisation, developments in DG technology, constraints on the construction of new transmission lines, increased customer demand for highly reliable electricity, and concerns about climate change. Government policies in several OECD countries already aim to increase the role of CHP in electricity production.

Distributed generation, through CHP plants or by renewable sources, also could have an important role in improving energy efficiency and reducing greenhouse-gas emissions. Various estimates suggest that CHP can reduce greenhouse-gas emissions from power generation and associated generation by 20%-30% compared with separate fossil-fired power and heating systems. Supplying power directly to consumers also avoids transmission and distribution losses, which average 6.8% in the OECD, further increasing efficiency compared with central generation.

Figure 1

Distributed Generation in an Electricity Network

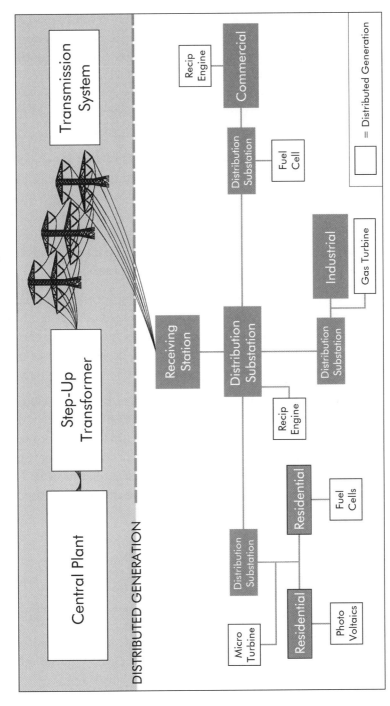

DISTRIBUTED GENERATION

☐ = Distributed Generation

Distributed generation is also a possible solution to constraints on the construction of new transmission lines. The rate of transmission-line construction has slowed in a number of OECD countries[2]. Although market liberalisation is increasing interest in expanding transmission interconnections, the ability to do so has been limited for environmental reasons. Growth in regional electricity demand might be met more easily by increases in distributed generation.

Electricity-market liberalisation is affecting distributed generation in two ways. New suppliers are identifying substantial niche markets where DG can be profitably deployed, such as enhancing reliability, peak clipping, and combined power and heating or cooling. Liberalised markets also put a premium on flexibility, an area where DG technologies, with their comparatively small size and short lead times, have a substantial advantage over large central plants.

Substantial technical advances are also increasing interest in distributed generation. New DG technologies, such as microturbines, are being introduced, while older technologies, such as reciprocating engines, have been improved. Fuel cells, which are being developed primarily for transportation applications, are a potential technology for the future.

Distributed generation has also faced difficulties in some countries as a result of liberalisation. In 2000, the European CHP association, Cogen Europe, published a report arguing that with the fall in electricity prices since market opening, CHP was at risk from "unfettered market liberalisation without regard to other policy objectives"[3]. New electricity-market arrangements in the UK have also been criticised for hampering distributed generators.

Investors in distributed generation face several regulatory barriers to the development and operation of DG. These include onerous technical requirements for interconnection, high charges for backup power and other ancillary services, and difficulties in obtaining siting permits, since some regulations do not take into account the relatively small scale of DG technologies.

---

2. *IEA, 2002.*
3. *Cogen Europe, 2000.*

Many OECD governments and regulators are studying these issues. The key remaining challenge is designing a framework that fully reflects the costs and benefits of DG to the economy, environment and energy security. The wide diversity of DG technologies makes it impossible to generalise about these costs and benefits.

Over the longer term, improved technologies or continued favourable government policies could ensure more widespread use of distributed generation. But distributed generation has been described as a "disruptive technology" that could fundamentally alter the organisation of the electricity-supply industry[4]. The arrival of DG on a large scale could herald a third generation of power sector reform[5]. The first generation of reform created independent power producers selling power to utilities, and the second created wholesale and retail markets. The third generation would provide for the widespread deployment of power generation directly at the sites of customers. As a result, electricity networks would operate in a much more decentralised manner. More power would be generated and managed by the system operator at low voltages. In such a system, the high-voltage network would backup the local decentralised systems. This decentralised network design would, however, require profound changes in the way the electricity networks are organised, constructed, and operated.

This study has three main objectives:

■ Survey the economic and regulatory status of distributed generation in selected OECD countries.

■ Examine the implications of wider deployment of various DG technologies on the market, environment, and energy security, as well as on the operation of electricity transmission and distribution networks.

■ Make general recommendations on accommodating distributed generation in liberalised electricity markets..

---

4. Dunn, S. 2000.
5. See, for example, Lonnroth, M. 1989

DISTRIBUTED-GENERATION TECHNOLOGIES

This chapter discusses the principal distributed-generation technologies in use in the OECD today. Diesel or gas reciprocating engines and gas turbines make up most of the capacity being installed. At the same time that new DG technologies such as microturbines are being introduced, older technologies such as reciprocating engines have been improved. Fuel cells are seen as a potential technology for the future. The costs of photovoltaic systems, while still high, are expected to continue falling over the next decade. Table I lists the various distributed-generation technologies and their estimated costs.

Reciprocating Engines

Reciprocating engines are the most common technology used for distributed generation. They are a proven technology with low capital cost, large size range, fast start-up capability, relatively high electric conversion efficiency (up to 43% for large diesel systems), and good operating reliability. These characteristics, combined with the engines' ability to start up during a power outage, make them the main choice for emergency or standby power supplies. They are by far the most commonly used power generation equipment under 1 MW.

Two types of engines are used. Gas-powered engines are mainly operated with natural gas, although biogas or landfill gas can also be used. Diesel engines can use diesel fuel, but can also be operated on other petroleum products such as heavy fuel oil or biodiesel.

An annual worldwide survey of orders for power-generating engines indicates that 16.2 GW of reciprocating engines (1-30 MW) were ordered from June 2000 to May 2001. Approximately 80% of the orders came from OECD countries. Most of them used oil fuel. Approximately half of total capacity was for emergency or standby service[6].

---

6. See DTGW, 2001.

Table 1

Distributed-Generation Technology Data

Technology	Diesel Engine	Gas Engine	Gas Turbine	Micro-turbine	Fuel cell	Photo-voltaic
Size (kW)	20-10 000 +	50-5 000 +	1 000 +	30-200	50-1 000 +	1 +
Efficiency (%)	36-43	28-42	21-40	25-30	35-54	n.a.
Generator cost (USD/kW)	125-300	250-600	300-600	500-750	1 500-3 000	n.a.
Turnkey cost (USD/kW)	350-500	600-1 000	650-900	1 000-1 300	1 900-3 500	5 000-7 000
Heat recovery cost (USD/kW)	n.a.	75-150	100-200	200-600	included	n.a.
O&M cost (USD/MWh)	5-10	7-15	3-8	5-10	5-10	1-4
CO_2 emissions (kg/MWh)	650	500-620	580-680	720	430-490	0
NO_x emissions (kg/MWh)	10	0.2-1.0	0.3-0.5	0.1	0.005-0.01	0

Notes: n.a. = not applicable. Turnkey cost includes associated electrical equipment for network interconnection but excludes additional costs for heat recovery. Sources: Gas Research Institute, The Role of Distributed Generation in Competitive Energy Markets, March 1999; emissions data from Expected Emissions Output from Various Distributed Generation Technologies, Regulatory Assistance Project, May 2001 (www.rapmaine.org).

The main drawbacks of reciprocating engines are noise, costly maintenance and high emissions, particularly of nitrogen oxides. These emissions can be reduced, with a loss of efficiency, by changing combustion characteristics. Catalytic converters are a proven emissions-control technology. Larger systems can use selective catalytic reduction (SCR) to reduce emissions. Particulate emission control is usually necessary with diesel engines.

Gas Turbines

Originally developed for jet engines, gas turbines of all sizes are now widely used in the power industry. Small industrial gas turbines of 1-20 MW are commonly used in CHP applications. They are particularly useful when higher temperature steam is required than can be produced by a reciprocating engine. The maintenance cost is slightly lower than for reciprocating engines, but so is the electrical conversion efficiency.

In the annual power-generation survey referred to above, gas turbines under 30 MW accounted for 4.3 GW of capacity ordered worldwide, with the majority coming from OECD countries.

Gas turbines can be noisy. Emissions are somewhat lower than for engines, and cost-effective NO_x emissions-control technology is commercially available.

Microturbines

Microturbines extend gas-turbine technology to smaller scales. The technology was originally developed for transportation applications, but is now finding a niche in power generation. One of the most striking technical characteristics of microturbines is their extremely high rotational speed. The turbine rotates up to 120 000 rpm and the generator up to 40 000 rpm. Individual units range from 30-200 kW but can be combined readily into systems of multiple units. Low combustion temperatures can assure very low NO_x emissions levels. They make much less noise than an engine of comparable size. Natural gas is expected to be the most common fuel, but flare gas, landfill gas, or biogas can also be used.

The main disadvantages of microturbines at this stage are its short track record and high costs compared with gas engines. The technology has been commercialised only recently and is offered by a small number of suppliers. Recent rises in natural gas prices and decreases in electricity prices have shifted marketing of these products "from a global market to niche applications"[7] such as burning flare gas at remote locations or landfill sites[8]. Significant cost reductions are likely to be made as manufacturing volume increases.

Fuel Cells

Fuel cells are compact, quiet power generators that use hydrogen and oxygen to make electricity. The transportation sector is the major potential market for fuel cells, and car manufacturers are making substantial investments in research and development. Power generation, however, is seen as a market in which fuel cells could be commercialised much more quickly.

Fuel cells can convert fuels to electricity at very high efficiencies (35%-60%), compared with conventional technologies. Their efficiency limits the emissions of greenhouse gases. As there is no combustion, other noxious emissions are low. Fuel cells can operate with very high reliability and so could supplement or replace grid-based electricity.

Only one fuel-cell technology for power plants, a phosphoric acid fuel-cell plant (PAFC), is currently commercially available. This plant has an output of 200 kW with a conversion efficiency of approximately 37%. Capital costs are approximately USD4 500 per kW, according to the manufacturer[9]. Over 200 have been ordered, for total worldwide installed capacity of over 40 MW.

---

7. *Courcelle, B. 2001.*
8. *Gillette, S. 2001.*
9. *www.internationalfuelcells.com*

Three other types of fuel cells, molten carbonate (MCFC), proton-exchange membrane (PEMFC)[10], and solid oxide (SOFC), are the focus of intensive research and development. The PEMFC is a low-temperature fuel cell and currently the leading choice for transportation applications. The PEMFC is also being tested for power generation. An early field-trial plant of approximately 200 kW yielded conversion efficiencies of approximately 34%. The MCFC is a high-temperature fuel cell with efficiencies estimated at 50-55%. It is expected that the MCFC will prove to be more economical in sizes above 1 MW. The SOFC is also a high-temperature fuel cell with similar efficiencies. Several companies plan to commercialise a household-size fuel cell (with a capacity of a few kW) in the next few years.

Fuel cells require a source of hydrogen as fuel. Most fuel cells currently under development plan to use hydrogen "reformed" (derived from) from natural gas, although in the future other sources of hydrogen could be used. The reformation process does produce limited emissions of NO_x and of carbon dioxide.

Photovoltaic Systems

Unlike the other DG technologies discussed above, photovoltaic systems are a capital-intensive, renewable technology with very low operating costs. They generate no heat and are inherently small-scale. These characteristics suggest that PV systems are best suited to household or small commercial applications, where power prices on the grid are highest.

According to the IEA's Photovoltaic Power Systems Programme, the installation cost of a basic photovoltaic system ranges from USD5 000 to USD7 000 per peak kW[11]. Operating costs are very low, as there are no fuelling costs. However, capacity factors are also low, ranging from 10% Germany to 22% in California. Although PV operates during daylight hours when demand (and generally prices) for power are higher, changing weather conditions affect its output.

---

10. *Sometimes referred to as a solid polymer fuel cell (SPFC).*
11. *Bulk purchases of PV systems for grid use can reduce these costs.*

Photovoltaic technology has a wide range of applications. About half of the existing PV systems in the OECD are off-grid. Stand-alone photovoltaic systems can be less expensive than extending power lines. Most of the currently profitable applications are remote telecommunications systems, where reliability and low maintenance are the principal requirements. PV systems also are widely used in developing countries, serving rural populations that have no other access to basic energy services. PV systems can be used to provide electricity for a variety of applications in households, community lighting, small businesses, agriculture, healthcare, and water supply.

The other half of existing PV capacity is on-grid, mostly as distributed generation. Most on-grid PV installations to date have enjoyed very large investment subsidies or favourable prices for the electricity they generate. The economic viability of PV systems is much higher when they can displace an extension to a distribution line.

Wind

Wind generation is rapidly growing in importance as a share of worldwide electricity supply. About 4.2 GW of capacity was installed during the year 2000[12]. Wind power is sometimes considered to be distributed generation, because the size and location of some wind farms makes it suitable for connection at distribution voltages. However, investments in wind power today are increasingly made in large wind farms by generating companies rather than by individual power consumers. In this sense, wind power is more like central generation than distributed generation as discussed above. Wind is not considered as distributed generation for the purposes of this report.

The variability of wind-farm output is, however, an issue that has become relevant to the operation of transmission and distribution networks. Market liberalisation has drawn attention to the costs imposed by this variability on power systems and the charges imposed on wind producers as a result.

---

12. IEA Wind, 2001.

Impact on the Market for Generating Equipment

Engines and turbines currently make up most of the orders for DG capacity. In 2000, orders for over 20 GW of engines and gas turbines (ranging from 1-30 MW[13]) accounted for around 10% of global electrical generating capacity orders. Although nearly half of these orders were for standby units, most of the remainder – over 8 GW – was for continuous use. Another 3.5 GW was for peaking capacity (Figure 2). While DG capacity has a relatively small share of the market compared with some other technologies – gas turbines (including combined cycles) accounted for two-thirds of orders – it is still much larger than the 4.3 GW of nuclear capacity that began construction during the year.

Figure 2

Orders for Engines and Turbines, 1-30 MW, for Peaking or Continuous Use, 1998/99 – 2000/01

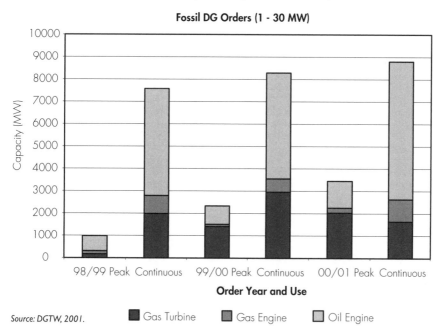

Source: DGTW, 2001.

---

13. Source: DGTW, 2001.

ECONOMICS OF DISTRIBUTED GENERATION

An evaluation of the economics of distributed generation must take into account:

■ The cost of electricity produced by DG versus the cost of delivered electricity from the grid.

■ The "option value" of DG to reduce costs and risks associated with energy consumption and production.

■ The value of any electricity exported from the DG project to the distribution grid.

■ The value of any ancillary services, reduced congestion on the distribution grid, or the costs of any increased network investment that may result from a DG project.

■ The value of the flexibility of DG technologies.

■ The value of other services that DG can offer customers, including greater electric reliability or CHP.

Distributed Generation Versus Central Power

The biggest potential market for distributed generation is displacing power supplied through the transmission and distribution grid. On-site power production circumvents transmission and distribution costs for the delivery of electricity. These costs average about 30% of the total cost of electricity. This share, however, varies according to customer size. For very large customers taking power directly at transmission voltage, the total cost and percentage are much smaller; for a small household consumer, network charges may constitute over 40% of the price.

Distributed generation has other economic advantages for particular customers. For example, customers with sizeable heat loads may produce both heat and power economically. Some customers have access to low cost fuel (such as landfill gas or local biomass), compared with commercially delivered fuel (which usually has a higher unit cost than for large central generators).

Distributed generation can also encourage greater competition in electricity supply, allowing even customers without DG greater choice in suppliers.

On the other hand, small-scale generation has a few direct cost disadvantages over central generation. First, there is a more limited selection of fuels and technologies to generate electricity – oil, natural gas, or photovoltaic systems, and, in certain cases, biomass or waste fuels. Second, the smaller generators used in DG cost more per kilowatt to build than larger plants used in central generation. Third, the costs of fuel delivery are normally higher. Finally, unless run in CHP mode, the smaller plants used in DG operate at lower fuel-conversion efficiencies than those of larger plants of the same type used in central generation.

Figure 3

Ratio of Industrial Fuel to Electricity Prices in Selected Countries

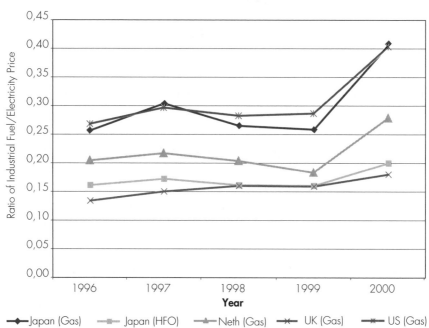

Source: based on data from IEA 2001a.

For fossil-fired distributed generation, its ability to compete with grid electricity depends on the ratio of the cost of fuel purchased to the cost of electricity to the consumer. These costs vary greatly from country to country. As this ratio falls, the cost attractiveness of fossil-fired DG improves. Figures 3 and 4 show this ratio for industrial and for domestic consumers for the four countries studied in this report (Japan, the Netherlands, the UK and the US) from 1996 to 2000. For all countries, the ratio of the price of gas (in USD per toe) has been divided by the price of electricity (also in USD per toe). For Japan, a comparison using fuel oil is also shown, since unlike other OECD countries, the cost of fuel oil is lower than the cost of LNG.

Figure 4

Ratio of Household Fuel to Electricity Prices in Selected Countries

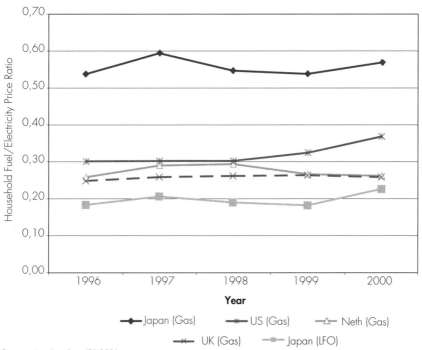

Source: using data from IEA 2001a.

The ratio also indicates the conversion efficiency of the distributed generator at which its cost of fuel equals the cost of the electricity replaced. For example, in the Netherlands in 2000, the fuel cost of an industrial generator running a DG plant at 28% efficiency would barely offset the cost of purchased power from the grid.

The figures show important differences in the ratio among countries, years – and fuels in the case of Japan. Perhaps the most striking difference is that Japan (for LNG) and the United States both consistently have the highest ratios, indicating that gas-fired DG in those countries is less economically feasible. By contrast, the UK and the Netherlands both have much lower ratios, suggesting that DG production is likely to be more viable. In 2000, as both fuel prices rose and electricity prices fell, the ratio increased sharply for all countries, except the UK. Further increases in gas prices in 2001 have exacerbated this trend. As for Japan, the figures illustrate that fuel-oil DG in Japan is much more viable compared with distributed generation from natural gas.

The total cost of generating electricity per kWh depends on a number of factors, particularly:

■ the cost of fuel, accounting for 50%-80% of the total cost per kilowatt hour;

■ the cost of the capital investment, making up 15%-35%; and

■ the capacity factor of the equipment.

Operating and maintenance costs, 10%-15% of total generating costs, are of secondary significance. Table 2 estimates of the cost of generation for various DG technologies for industrial consumers. (It is very difficult make precise calculations because of the different sizes of the equipment and variations in fuel costs within and between countries.) For household consumers, generation costs will be 4-6 U.S. cents per kWh higher because of higher fuel-delivery costs.

■ Economics of Photovoltaic Electricity

The economics of photovoltaic technology is almost the opposite of other technologies used in distributed generation. PV systems have high capital costs, but no fuel costs and modest operating costs.

Table 2

Indicative Costs of Various
Distributed-Generation Technologies

Distributed-Generation Technology	Indicative Cost of Generation Industrial (U.S. cents/kWh) at 60% Load Factor
Diesel Engine	7-11
Gas Engine	6-9
Gas Turbine	6-9
Microturbine	7-9
Fuel Cell	11-14

The competitiveness of PV power, compared with grid electricity, also must take into account the cost of electricity and the location of the PV installation. PV systems in sunny locations in lower latitudes (such as California) produce nearly twice as much power annually as in northern Europe. While fossil-fired distributed generation reduces the customer's exposure to volatile electricity prices, PV reduces exposure to volatile electricity *and* fuel prices.

Due to its high capital cost alone, however, PV is currently uncompetitive for grid applications, unless it is subsidised. The lines on Figure 5 illustrate the break-even electricity prices of PV at different capacity factors. The dots show the current household retail prices and capacity factors for the four countries in this study. For the US, the state of California is used; it is a best case that has both high capacity factors and high electricity prices. The figure shows that PV costs need to be reduced by at least a factor of two for California and Japan, and by much more for the Netherlands and the UK, before the technology becomes remotely competitive at displacing grid-based power for household use in OECD countries.

■ Flexibility Increases the Value of Distributed Generation

Conventional cost assessments of generating options tend to understate the value of flexibility to the owner of generating plant.

Figure 5

Comparison of PV Costs/Output to Household Electricity Rates in Selected OECD Countries

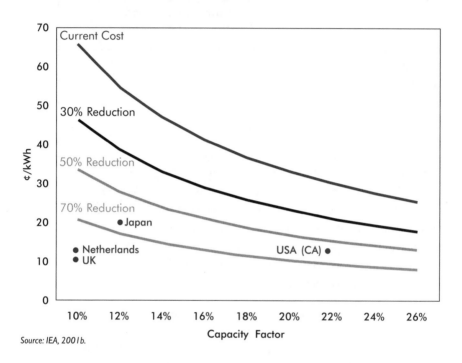

Source: IEA, 2001b.

Many DG technologies are flexible in operation, size, and expandability. A distributed generator can respond to price incentives reflected in fluctuating fuel and electricity prices. When fuel prices are high and electricity prices are low, the distributed generator purchases from the electricity market. In the opposite situation, the producer supplies to the market. In other words, the availability of on-site power is a physical hedge for the customer against volatility in electricity prices. Many distributed generators in Japan operate in precisely this fashion, displacing power from the grid only during peak periods and meeting all their needs from the grid off-peak.

A distributed generator can expand generating capacity more readily than a central generator and may be able to do so quickly in response to a rapid increase in demand – created by inadequate generation, transmission, or distribution – depending on the configuration and the size of the interconnection. Modular generating plants can be ordered and installed in weeks. Distribution utilities already use combustion-turbine units installed at distribution substations for this purpose.

Market liberalisation greatly increases the flexibility of the distributed generator. In a captive market, a distributed generator may not be allowed to export power to the network or may be permitted to sell only to the local distributor. In a liberalised market, the excess can be sold to any consumer in the same distribution network. That ability may allow the distributed generator to justify the purchase of a larger generating plant, which can lower unit capital and operating costs. The liberalised market also allows distributed generators to contract with other producers for backup electricity. The ability to source backup power competitively should reduce costs of this source of supply.

The flexibility of distributed generation is difficult to assess but may be very important in determining its overall value. "Real option valuation" is attracting increased interest in the field of power generation, in part because it attempts to value the flexibility of different types of generating plants in volatile market conditions. Recent work in this area suggests that flexible power plants operating during peak periods may be much more profitable than conventional evaluations suggest[14]. Fossil-fired DG has similar characteristics and thus should have similar option values. While some distributed generation is clearly flexible in operation, other forms, e.g. PV or CHP where output is determined by the heat load, have limited operational flexibility. The Edison Electric Institute has published a study using real options to estimate the value of the grid interconnection to the distributed generator[15].

---

14. Frayer J., and N. Uludere, 2001.

15. Pati, M., Ristau, R., Sheblé, G. and M. Wilhelm, 2001.

■ Distributed Generation Can Provide Grid Benefits

Distributed generators, depending on location, may offer additional value to the grid:

■ **Deferral of upgrades to the transmission system.** When a transmission system is congested, an appropriately located DG can reduce the congestion and thus can defer the need for an upgrade, particularly when the growth in congestion is low[16].

■ **Deferral of upgrades to the distribution system.** If a distribution network is operating near capacity or needs to be upgraded to accommodate power flows from the generator, DG installed at a transformer station, for example, may allow a distribution company to cope with the problem, delaying the need to upgrade distribution assets.

■ **Reduction of losses in the distribution system.** System losses are affected by changes in power flows in the distribution network. On-site generation will cut system losses by reducing power demand on the system. Furthermore, if a distributed generator is located near a large load, then its exported power will also tend to cut system losses. In contrast, power exported to the grid from remote distributed generators may increase these system losses.

■ **Provision of network support or ancillary services[17].** The connection of distributed generators to networks generally leads to a rise in voltage in the network. In areas where voltage support is difficult, installation of a distributed generator may improve quality of supply.

A full evaluation of the economics of distributed generation must determine whether its benefits to the grid are passed on to the producer. This question is discussed in more detail in the policy chapter.

---

16. See Chapel, S. and C. Feinstein, 2000.

17. Ancillary services include provision of reserve power, controlling the frequency and voltage of electricity, and reactive power.

Combined Heat and Power (CHP)

The combination of heat with power generation is a well-established type of distributed generation. Most CHP generating capacity meets demand for process heat in larger industries, particularly the iron and steel, chemical, refining, pulp and paper, and food-processing industries. Most of the rest, which includes process heat as well as district heating, is either used in smaller industries or in buildings. Surplus power, normally sold to the local utility, can then be exported to the electricity network.

Integrating heat production with power production only slightly increases capital costs (less than 10% for industrial systems). Those costs can be more than offset by the value of heat energy produced. For example, UK projects have an average electricity conversion efficiency of 20% and utilise a further 51% as heat. The size of the CHP system matters: the most cost-effective match the heat load.

As with other technologies, there are significant economies of scale. For example, a CHP system using a 100 kW engine costs about 60% per kilowatt than one with a 3 MW engine. The most economically attractive CHP technology up to a few MW is usually gas engines and at the larger sizes, steam turbines. At this stage, CHP using microturbines is not competitive; it has somewhat higher capital costs and lower overall efficiencies compared with gas engines. Fuel cells are much further from being commercially competitive but do offer the advantage of higher electrical efficiencies.

Because of the significant capital investment, CHP is more economically attractive at high utilisation rates. UK systems operate at a moderately high capacity factor of 57%, even though many of them run at part load nearly continuously. However, in countries with a significant amount of district heating, overall capacity factors in CHP mode are much lower.

The cost-effectiveness of CHP facilities are more site-specific than for other DG projects because of the need to find customers with a need for heat. At the industrial level, experience in Denmark and the

Table 3

Capital Costs and Efficiencies of CHP Technologies

Type	Size (MW)	Installed Cost (USD/kW)	Electrical Efficiency	Overall Efficiency
Micro-CHP (Stirling Engine)	< 0.015	2 700	15-25%	85-95%
Microturbine	0.1	1 970	28.7%	59%
Engine	0.1	1 380	28.1%	75%
Fuel Cell	0.2	3 764	36.0%	73%
Engine	0.8	975	30.9%	65%
Engine	3	850	33.6%	62%
Turbine	1	1 600	21.9%	72%
Turbine	5	1 075	27.6%	73%
Turbine	10	965	29.0%	74%
Turbine	25	770	34.3%	78%
Turbine	40	700	37.0%	78%

Source: Onsite Sycom 2000b and c; Future Cogen, 2001 (micro-CHP).

Netherlands shows that payback time is crucial to the investment decision. The payback is considered prohibitive in excess of 4-5 years[18].

The growth in CHP in OECD countries is largely due to favourable government and regulatory policies[19]. These policies have taken the form of investment tax credits and national targets for electricity from CHP, obligations on the electric utility to purchase CHP power, favourable prices for fuel or ancillary services provided to the CHP project, and favourable electricity prices for CHP power (in some cases supported by government subsidies). As a result, CHP generating capacity has continued to grow despite overcapacity in some countries. The policies have also encouraged CHP systems to produce a higher proportion of power for the grid than if based only on the heat load.

18. See NEA/IEA 1998, Annex 4.

19. Finland is a notable exception where substantial CHP capacity has been constructed and operated without major subsidies.

In the European Union[20], CHP accounted for 72 GW of capacity and 11% of total electricity generated in 1998, although the share varied greatly from 1.9% in Ireland to 62.3% in Denmark. In a 1997 communication, the European Commission proposed a community strategy to promote CHP to increase energy efficiency and reduce greenhouse-gas emissions. It said that a doubling of CHP from its 1994 level of 9% to 18% was "realistically achievable" but required Member states to remove various obstacles to CHP[21].

Four industries (chemical, refining, food, and pulp and paper) account for 80% of industrial CHP in the EU. And industry as a whole accounts for 80% of total CHP. Most CHP capacity is large and tends to be connected at high voltages (i.e. 110 kV or above)[22].

---

20. *Data problems make detailed analysis of CHP very difficult. The statistical information is often incomplete and not always comparable because of differences in definitions. The IEA collects data on heat sold to third parties. The heat that CHP units provide for consumption in place is not reported in IEA data as part of the output of the CHP unit. This report relies on national sources and on Eurostat. However, quantitative comparisons between countries must be made with caution.*

21. *EC, 1997.*

22. *Eurostat, the European statistical body, recently adopted a new methodology for calculating CHP, starting with the 1999 statistics. The new methodology uses a stricter definition of CHP, which may result in lower estimates of CHP capacity.*

Table 4

European Union CHP 1998

Member State	CHP generating capacity (MW)	CHP Electricity (GWh)	Share of total electricity production (%)
Austria	3 416	14 268	24.8
Belgium	797	3 410	4.1
Denmark	7 027	25 591	62.3
Finland	5 097	25 128	35.8
France	3 485	12 660	2.5
Germany	22 160	41 770	7.5
Greece	257	981	2.1
Ireland	114	404	1.9
Italy	9 802	45 990	17.8
Luxembourg	98	320	22.5
Netherlands	8 500	47 835	52.6
Portugal	965	3 288	8.4
Spain	3 558	21 916	11.2
Sweden	3 205	9 544	6.0
United Kingdom	3 842	20 759	5.8
EU-15	72 323	273 864	11.0

Source: Eurostat.

In the United States, CHP provides 50.4 GW, or about 6% of total electrical generating capacity. Industrial CHP accounts for about 90% of all CHP. As in the European Union, 80% of industrial CHP is present in the same four industries.

Japan's CHP installations, known as "cogeneration systems", have total capacity of 5 GW, accounting for 2% of power production. Nearly 80% of this capacity is installed in the industrial sector.

■ Most CHP is Large CHP

In the US and the UK, large installations account for most of the CHP capacity. In the US, CHP plants greater than 10 MW account for nearly half of the total and 97% of all CHP capacity. UK statistics show that while CHP units over 10 MW make up only 5% of the total, they represent over 78% of CHP capacity.

■ Small CHP Applications

Small CHP plants, those producing under 10 MW, to date contribute little to overall CHP capacity. They are less cost-effective due to higher unit capital costs and more limited requirements for heating in the commercial sector. Recent growth in the EU has been slow[23]. However, CHP may be a viable option for commercial consumers whose electricity prices are much higher than for industrial consumers. Gas engines and microturbines can be easily sized for this market. Fuel cells have the same potential. Japan, for example, has been an early adopter of DG technologies in the commercial sector in response to high electricity prices.

■ Combining Cooling with Power Generation Can be Economically Attractive in the Commercial Sector

The demand for cooling represents a large portion of peak electrical load and a substantial large share of electricity consumption in many OECD countries. It is a particularly important electrical load in the commercial sector. Although electrical chillers provide nearly all the cooling today, gas-absorption chilling is a viable alternative where needs are large, such as in the commercial sector and for some industrial applications. A gas-absorption cooling system running on waste heat from on-site power generation can be even more economically attractive. Some new buildings – particularly "Internet hotels" housing computer hardware for Web sites – have both high cooling and power loads, i.e. 20-30 MW compared with 5 MW for a hospital. Those buildings are installing combined systems as the most economical way of meeting these needs as well as providing increased reliability. The NY Cybercentre in New York City will have a "trigeneration"

---

23. See SAVE, 2001.

system (combining power generation, heating and cooling) with generating capacity of 47 MW and chilling capacity of 16 000 tons for its 37 000 m^2 of office space[24].

The market penetration of gas-absorption cooling technology in the commercial sector is limited to these special applications because of higher capital costs (approximately 50% over a conventional electrical chiller), the larger size of the chilling equipment, and limited familiarity with the technology.

■ Household CHP Technologies are being Commercialised

Nearly all CHP applications to date have been developed for either the industrial or commercial sectors. Development of CHP systems for the household market – micro-CHP systems as they are commonly called – has been largely neglected because of high unit costs.

Recent technological developments with gas-fired engines, however, have made household systems economically viable. They can be operated to provide all home-heating needs (for hydronic heating systems); electricity is produced as a by-product. Some systems have attained electricity-only efficiencies of 12%-25% and overall heat utilisation rates of up to 90%.

A number of companies have announced plans to commercialise engine-based micro-CHP for household use. Costs of an installed system vary widely because the technological is in an early stage but are estimated at USD1 300-USD1 500 per kW. Total operating hours depend on the climate, of course, but are likely to be 2 000 – 4 000 hours annually in Europe. If all the electrical output from the system can displace grid power, the payback period is as short as four years.

---

24. Perrault, L. 2001.

Fuel cells are the other major technology being explored for household CHP use. The domestic market for power generation is seen as one of the first for fuel-cell technology. Costs on the domestic market are less of a constraint than on the automotive market, for example, even though a fuel-cell CHP system would be much more expensive than an engine-based system. Several companies, including automotive companies, electric utilities as well as smaller firms, have announced intentions to market fuel cells as domestic power generators within the next few years.

Several attempts have been made to forecast the market for micro-CHP. One assessment concludes that the European market will experience very rapid growth – up to half a million units annually from 2003 to 2010. Germany, the UK, the Netherlands, Italy, Austria, and Switzerland are likely to be the biggest markets[25]. The study also predicts slower penetration of Asian and North American markets because of the warmer climate in Asia and because hydronic heating systems in North America are less common.

Significant barriers remain to be overcome before the market grows that quickly. The most important is the high initial cost of household CHP systems compared with that of conventional boilers. Sales of more efficient condensing domestic boilers in the UK, for example, are very low despite a small price premium (about USD200 or 15% over conventional boilers) and payback periods of 3-4 years. As the price of a household CHP system is two to three times higher than a regular gas boiler, it is difficult to imagine that consumers will accept the higher initial investment. A more promising route to commercialisation may be leasing and installation of the systems by third parties.

As some systems may need to export power to the grid, a second barrier is related to costs and possibilities for doing so. The main additional costs involve the grid interconnection. The feasibility of selling small amounts of power in a liberalised market is discussed further in the policy chapter.

---

25. *See Huhn, K. 2001.*

Reliability, and Standby or Emergency Power

The most important application of distributed generation today is as emergency power. More than 100 GW of diesel generating capacity is available in the US alone[26]. Over 70% of that is estimated to be for standby or emergency use. The existence of this largely neglected source of grid power is gaining increased attention, particularly in the United States where demand growth has led to tighter capacity margins. In the summer of 2001, system operators in New Mexico and Oregon arranged for the use of existing standby generators to supply additional power to the grid under emergency conditions. Electric utilities have co-ordinated the operation of these standby generators through communications networks and software that permit the utilities to remotely operate the standby generators as needed[27].

Distributed generation is also used by distribution utilities to deal with local network congestion problems resulting from load growth. By moving portable power generators (usually portable diesel generators or combustion turbines powered by natural gas) to distribution substations, utilities have been able to cope with rapid load growth more quickly than by upgrading distribution facilities.

A new application for DG is supplying companies for which outages from the local electricity grid would be very expensive. These companies include those in industries that use continuous manufacturing processes (chemicals, petroleum refining, paper, metals, and others) and those that provide essential services. They particularly include so-called "digital economy" industries like telecommunications, data storage and retrieval, and financial companies.

Table 5 shows estimated costs of a one-hour power outage for selected US businesses. A recent survey of US manufacturers and "digital economy" companies underscored the expenses of even short outages. The average cost of a one-hour outage was USD7 795 and USD1 477 for a *one-second* outage[28].

---

26. *Singh, V. 2001.*
27. *Peltier, R., 2001.*
28. *Primen, 2001.*

Table 5

Cost of a One-hour Power Outage for Different US Businesses

Industry	Hourly outage cost (USD)
Cellular communications	41 000
Telephone ticket sales	72 000
Airline reservations	90 000
Credit card operations	2 580 000
Brokerage operations	6 480 000

Source: US Department of Energy.

Companies are investing in the key area of preventing power losses to their computers. A simple uninterrupted power supply (UPS) system using capacitors or batteries to protect a network server costs a few hundred USD. With such a system, the server can survive a short disruption and safely back up information before the UPS batteries are depleted. While the cost of a UPS battery system may seem high compared with bulk electricity supply in USD per kW or USD per MWh, it is inexpensive compared with the cost of the server, lost data, and productivity.

As a consequence, demand has been growing for higher reliability in electricity supply. An oft-cited standard for highly reliable power is "six nines" of reliability (i.e. 99.9999%), equivalent to 30 seconds of outage per year. As most outages are caused by the distribution system, on-site protection is the only feasible solution. Two DG technologies could provide such protection: backup systems combined with UPS systems and fuel cells. A gas-engine backup system combined with a flywheel UPS system recently has been commercialised. A US bank clearinghouse has installed four fuel cells as part of a UPS system to ensure nearly continuous operation (outage time of 1 second per year). The Harvard Medical School, where a single outage could lead to the loss of years of research, is considering a power system based on fuel cells[29].

---

29. See Milford, L. 2001.

Reliability concerns are fuelling the purchase of DG generating capacity. While this capacity is a tiny share of overall electricity production, it can be expected to become an increasingly important source of peak supply. In this way, distributed generation is contributing to the security of electricity supply.

Offgrid and Remote Consumers

Service to customers not connected to the main electricity grids is distributed generation. Although a relatively small percentage of consumers are served off-grid in the OECD[30], that share represents about half a million electricity consumers in the US, Canada, and Australia alone.

The main policy question regarding off-grid consumers is whether the grids should be expanded to serve these consumers. For the most part, grids already have been expanded where expansion has made economic sense. In liberalised markets, off-grid consumers generally do not have as many suppliers to choose from as on-grid consumers. The remoteness of these off-grid communities may impede competition and keep prices high in the local power grid.

Nevertheless, use of the latest DG technologies may reduce the premium that individual consumers in off-grid communities pay for a high-quality power supply. Hybrid systems, such as diesel-wind generators, are becoming increasingly viable options for utilities and individual consumers. Encouraging individual consumers to develop their own power supply also could enhance power reliability in these communities.

Pricing policy also influences the efficient development of the power supply to off-grid communities. A number of jurisdictions have pricing policies that set similar retail electricity rates for remote communities and grid-connected customers, for reasons of equity. However, these policies discourage local customers from developing their own supply.

---

30. *The issue is of great importance outside the OECD, where "offgrid" is more likely to imply no electricity service at all.*

Rescinding these policies would encourage greater investment in energy efficiency and in distributed generation.

Besides these community-sized applications, there are even smaller applications of off-grid DG technologies that are more cost-effective than grid power. Photovoltaic systems combined with battery storage can be the most economical method of powering low-capacity factor applications such as remote lighting and telephone service. These methods are obviously attractive when the application is distant from the distribution grid. But sometimes the cost alone of adding a single street light to a grid can exceed the capital cost of installing a PV-based lighting system. Falling costs for DG systems can be expected to result in their greater use for these niche applications.

DISTRIBUTED GENERATION IN JAPAN, THE US, THE NETHERLANDS, AND THE UK

The status of distributed generation differs in each OECD country. While economics is certainly a fundamental factor, as discussed in the previous chapters, other factors come into play. This chapter examines other influences on the development of distributed generation in the OECD, particularly market structure and electricity-market reform, and reviews policies in Japan, the United States, the Netherlands, and the United Kingdom.

Japan

The Japanese electricity industry consists of ten vertically integrated, privately owned utilities that serve virtually all electricity consumers. The total electrical generating capacity of approximately 253 GW produces 1 062 TWh of electric power generation.

Electricity prices in Japan are the highest of all OECD countries, reflecting high capital costs for generation, transmission and distribution equipment; high costs for land; and the moderately high cost of fossil fuels, particularly natural gas, which must be imported in liquefied form. High power prices account for a large proportion of industrial autoproduction of power in Japan. Over 30% of electricity consumption in the manufacturing sector is taken care of by on-site power production, which amounts to nearly 28 GW or 116 TWh of power consumption – 12% of total Japanese consumption[31]. Many of these large industrial plants generate electricity with coal. Approximately one-sixth of this industrial power production is supplied by cogeneration.

The electricity market has been partly liberalised in Japan. Extra-high voltage consumers, which represent 30% of electricity consumption,

---

31. *METI, 2001.*

have been able to choose suppliers since March 2000. To date, less than 1% of them have switched suppliers.

Because it is the most viable alternative to utility supply, distributed generation could be of interest to many electricity consumers. There are three common types: oil-fired capacity in "monogeneration" designed principally to clip peak demand, oil-fired CHP using diesel engines and steam turbines, and gas-fired CHP with engines, gas, or steam turbines. The high retail price of natural gas in Japan makes gas-fired monogeneration uneconomical (see Table 6). However, gas is the only option in Tokyo, Yokohama, and Osaka due to tight environmental regulations.

Table 6

Economics of Gas CHP in Japan

Type	Annual operation (hours)	Size of unit (kW)	Capital cost (USD/kW)	Fuel Cost (USD/kWh)	Value of Heat (USD/kWh)	Net generating costs (USD/kWh)	Retail electricity rate (USD/kWh)
Building	3 000	500	2 500	0.12	0.06	0.16	0.17
Factory	6 000	500	2 000	0.10	0.05	0.11	0.10
Factory	6 000	5 000	750	0.10	0.03	0.096	0.10

Source: METI (exchange rate 120 yen = USD1).

Complete statistics are not available on generation without CHP. A survey by the Japan Engine Generator Association (NEGA) estimates that of the 2 418 MW of distributed generation (excluding emergency power) installed from 1997 to 2000, approximately 40% was for non-CHP systems[32].

According to the Japan Cogeneration Centre, there are about 5 486 MW of cogeneration in Japan, of which 4 371 MW is industrial and 1 115 MW is commercial[33]. Industrial cogeneration systems generated 20.9 TWh of power in fiscal year 1999. Gas turbines and

---

32. NEGA, 2001.
33. CGC Japan, 2001.

diesel engines account for over 90% of the generators (see Table 7). Growth in cogeneration systems has been steady, averaging more than 360 MW a year since the late 1980s.

Table 7

Cogeneration System Capacity (in MW) by Sector and Generator Type as of March 2001

	Gas Turbine[34]	Gas Engine	Diesel Engine
Commercial	209	291	483
Industrial	2 252	186	1 552
Total	**2 461**	**477**	**2 035**

Source: Japan Cogeneration Centre.

Cogeneration in Japan benefits from:

■ investment incentives in the form of high depreciation or initial tax credit, plus low interest rate loans from the Development Bank of Japan, and;

■ subsidies up to 15% for major district heating and cooling projects. Monogeneration receives no subsidies.

In Japan, most cogeneration that is classified as "gas turbine" uses fuels other than natural gas (e.g. fuel oil, blast furnace gas, or refinery gas). METI, which considers cogeneration fired by natural gas to be a form of "new energy", forecasts it will grow from 1.52 GW of capacity in 1999 (excluding steam turbines) to 3.44 GW by 2010. With additional measures such as support for research, development, demonstration, and diffusion of the technologies, METI foresees 4.64 GW of capacity by 2010.

Charges for backup power for a customer using a DG system are substantial but less than regular capacity charges. Capacity charges are 10% above the normal rate when backup power is actually used. When backup is not needed, capacity charges for business are 30% of the normal rate (20% for industry). Energy charges for backup power are 10% above the normal rate for a scheduled outage and 25% above for an unscheduled one.

---

34. Includes gases other than natural gas.

Several firms are active in selling DG systems including Eneserve, Yanmar, and Mitsubishi Heavy Industries. A ten-year contract to build-own-operate (BOO) is the most common arrangement. Not surprisingly, some electric utilities have identified distributed generation as a new growth business. Tokyo Electric Power has created the new subsidiary "My Energy" to sell oil-fired engine systems to industrial and commercial consumers. As of March 2001, My Energy had signed contracts with 44 customers, 42 of them will use diesel engine generation[35]. My Energy achieved a notable first in Japan as the first utility affiliate to take a customer away from another (Tohoku Electric). Seven other utilities have also established similar subsidiaries. Leasing arrangements are becoming increasingly common.

Several regulatory barriers have been removed to encourage the development of distributed generation and cogeneration systems in particular. These include adjustments to fire regulations, the repeal of a requirement for an on-site electrical engineer, and reduced inspection requirements. The government also plans to eliminate the requirement for an on-site boiler engineer.

However, some regulatory barriers remain. Selling excess distributed generation to another electricity customer is generally not allowed, even though that ability would improve the cost-effectiveness of a number of projects. The requirements for electrical protection equipment, which add at least 10% to the total cost of the facility, could be simplified.

Another factor is the behaviour of utilities in the partly liberalised market. Although METI guidelines clearly state that utilities are not to impede the development of self-generation, suppliers of DG equipment have suggested that utilities discourage customers from developing their own distributed generation by selectively cutting their electricity rates.

A large potential market exists for natural gas cogeneration, particularly when combined with cooling in urban areas. Gas cogeneration and gas cooling together account for 45% of gas sales by

---

35. Hangai, E. 2001.

Tokyo Gas. They are expected to account for over half of the growth in the company's gas demand over the next five years. Future technical developments aim at producing more cost-effective systems for cogeneration and for gas cooling. Microturbine systems appear promising because of good environmental performance but will not be a viable option until the capital costs of CHP systems decline further.

In summary, distributed generation is already playing a role in Japan by applying competitive pressure, at least in selected market segments, on the utility market. It appears to be one reason that utilities have recently cut prices, since competition for liberalised consumers, particularly among utilities, has so far been very limited. DG could contribute to the electricity supply, however, with:

■ further market liberalisation, to allow more customers to choose, generate, and export energy; and

■ appropriate pricing of backup energy, transmission, and ancillary services.

If DG is to make a large contribution, however, its cost – through technological improvements and lower gas prices – must decline compared with the cost of grid electricity.

The United States

The US electric power system is very complex, representing the diverse federal nature of the country. Although more than 200 investor-owned utilities supply about three-quarters of customers, over 2 900 municipal and rural utilities supply the remaining quarter. Wholesale electricity markets are the responsibility of the federal government through its regulatory agency the Federal Energy Regulatory Commission, but retail commerce in electricity is the responsibility of the states.

This decentralised responsibility means that retail electricity-market liberalisation is proceeding at very different rates in different states. Although 23 states have enacted legislation to liberalise the electricity market, many others have indicated that they will not proceed with such reforms in the near future. Events in California have slowed reforms in several states.

Energy costs in the US are lower than in most OECD countries, both for electricity and for gas. Prices for these commodities, however, vary greatly across the country. The low cost of energy has limited the spread of distributed generation and particularly CHP, which accounts for 50.4 GW or about 6% of total electrical generating capacity. Industrial CHP accounts about 90% of all CHP. Of that share, 80% of existing industrial CHP is in four industries: paper, chemicals, petroleum refining, and food processing.

A large application for distributed generation is emergency power. Diesel emergency generators at industrial sites and commercial buildings account for over 100 GW of US generating capacity. Standby generators in California alone provide 3.2 GW of capacity, equivalent to over 6% of peak electricity demand in the state, according to a detailed survey by the California Energy Commission[36]. Electricity system operators in New York developed mechanisms to make this capacity – totalling 120 MW – available to supply peak loads during power emergencies[37]. The prospect of increased use of diesel generation has also increased concern about the associated emissions impact[38].

An analysis prepared for the US Department of Energy suggests that the market potential for CHP in the country is over 160 GW – 88 GW in the industrial sector and the rest in the commercial sector. The US Combined Heat and Power Association, in co-operation with the US Department of Energy and US Environmental Protection Agency, developed a "National CHP Roadmap" intended to double CHP capacity from 46 GW in 1998 to 92 GW by 2010[39].

The US Department of Energy is involved in a large research and development effort to promote distributed generation that considers all renewable resources. Its Distributed Energy Resources Strategic Plan[40] budgets USD279.9 million in fiscal year 2000 for R&D the areas

---

36. *CEC, 2001.*
37. *NYISO, 2001.*
38. *Singh, V. 2001.*
39. *USCHPA, 2001.*
40. *USDOE, 2000.*

of: technology development (PV, fuel cells, wind, geothermal, industrial power, and other solar), technology base (advanced engine materials and turbine technologies), systems architecture, and systems implementation (including integration of DG into grids).

The current administration under President George W. Bush has identified a need to expand generating capacity in the US. The National Energy Policy makes favourable references to encouraging CHP through tax incentives, encouraging development at existing industrial sites, and by encouraging greater flexibility in the environmental permitting process[41].

The main issues regarding distributed generation in the US are:

■ **A need to improve cost-effectiveness.** Relatively low electricity prices and recent spikes in natural gas prices limit the growth of distributed generation. The US Department of Energy estimates additional DG capacity by 2020 of 1.) 20 GW of CHP, 2.) 12.7 GW of "distributed generation" (primarily gas-fired peaking plants used by utilities), and 3.) 0.54 GW of solar PV[42]. Little new capacity is forecast for the commercial sector until 2015, when falling costs for fuel cells and microturbines, in particular, is expected to make these options competitive[43].

■ **Permitting processes.** The decentralised system of permitting in the US hinders siting approval.

■ **Variable interconnection standards.** There is not yet a national standard for interconnection of distributed generation to the network. Utilities lacking experience with DG may require stringent interconnection limits for small units that are more appropriate for larger units. Connection costs for DG projects vary, according to a study prepared for the National Renewable Energy Laboratory that looked at both fossil-fired and renewable DG. Many projects reported excess costs associated with the technical requirements of connection. One 500 kW cogeneration system project said the cost was

---

41. *National Energy Policy, p. 4-11.*
42. *EIA, 2000.*
43. *See EIA, 2001.*

USD1 000 per kW[44]. A national standard (IEEE P1547) is under development and may be adopted in 2002.

■ **Incomplete regulatory reform.** Many states have not liberalised their electricity markets. Many of those give utilities public service responsibilities such as supplier of last resort. Distributed generators generally have difficulty gaining the co-operation of distribution utilities. They report obstacles such as lack of access to the distribution system, high charges for backup power (up to USD200 per kW a year)[45], and utility price cuts to customers interested in installing their own generation. On the other hand, public and private utilities are concerned that customers generating their own electricity will lead to higher electricity rates. Some have argued that distributed generators should pay stranded costs.

■ **Environmental standards.** First, environmental regulations are made at the state or local level. Generating companies cannot easily persuade regulators to adopt a uniform standard. Second, some regulatory authorities have established standards based on emissions rate, in pounds per MWh for example, regardless of size. In Texas, air-quality regulators set the same standard for NO_x in high pollution areas for gas turbine with advanced NO_x control (SCR) – 2 ppm of NO_x or lower[46]. This cannot be achieved by a natural gas engine, even with SCR added. It barely can be achieved by a microturbine equipped with an SCR, but the cost of such a system is prohibitive. Such standards effectively rule out fossil-fuel DG.

■ **Technical limitations.** The greater use of radial grids in the US, compared with much of Europe, presents a technical challenge[47]. Radial grids are not designed to accommodate backward flows. Small utilities, especially, may find it difficult to handle distributed generation sent into the network. Heavy investments to upgrade distribution networks would be needed to accommodate large amounts of DG. Upgrading costs are normally passed onto the distributed generator.

---

44. *Alderfer, B., M. Eldridge and T. Starrs, 2000.*
45. *Alderfer, B., M. Eldridge and T. Starrs, 2000.*
46. *TNRCC, 2001.*
47. *Onsite Sycom, 2000a.*

The Netherlands

The Dutch electricity system is served by four generating companies that supply approximately half of the total electricity supply. Decentralised production accounted for nearly 40% and imports nearly 20% of the total in 1999. Over 60% of power production is from natural gas, which is produced domestically and is generally the most economical option for power generation.

The Dutch electricity sector is strongly influenced by the government's policies to reduce carbon-dioxide emissions and improve energy sustainability. The 1989 Electricity Act strongly encouraged market entry by decentralised combined heat and power for environmental reasons. A variety of incentives resulted in a doubling of CHP from 1990 including:

■ government investment subsidies of up to 17.5% (until 1995);

■ an obligation by generating companies to purchase surplus power generated from these facilities at the estimated full cost of new central generation facilities (also until 1995);

■ favourable natural gas prices from the 50% state-owned gas supplier Gasunie (until 2000); and

■ an exemption (until 1997) from paying for reserve capacity or ancillary services[48].

Growth in CHP created so much overcapacity that central generation output had to be curtailed to accommodate its surplus power.

In 1998, the government passed legislation to introduce market reforms to the electricity sector. A wholesale electricity market started operating the next year. A new network regulator, DTE, which regulates network charges, was created. Customers are being liberalised in stages; only small customers have yet to be liberalised. A new transmission company, TenneT, operates the transmission system. Distributors, which are owned by municipal and regional governments, have been obliged to separate their distribution

---

48. IEA, 2000.

businesses from other activities (including retailing electricity and joint ventures with customers on generation).

The presence of a large share of distributed generation in the Dutch system before the reform meant that the design of the electricity market had to take DG into account from the outset. The system operator, TenneT, co-ordinates the system and controls the central generators. Nevertheless, local network operators are actively involved in balancing their own systems (starting at 110 kV and below). They are able to cope with high levels of CHP without compromising reliability. Some operational problems have resulted from a lack of communication between TenneT and distributed producers, but are now uncommon.

The Netherlands feature a few industrial CHP producers that have formed their own "power parks". Each industrial CHP producer has its own generating capacity and connection to the grid, and also supplies power to other sites that are not connected to the grid.

Much of Dutch distributed generation is the result of investment by distributors in joint ventures with industry. As a result of the separation requirements of electricity-market liberalisation, the ownership and operation of CHP is now operationally separate from the ownership of the networks. Separation aids competition but prohibits investment by a distributor in generation to support the local network.

Interconnection issues are not generally a problem. A study by Cogen Europe comparing Dutch, French, and UK interconnection rules found that the Dutch rules were comparatively clear and transparent[49].

Market rules do incorporate some advantages for distributed generation:

■ While small distributed generation, of under 10 MVA does not have to pay connection or use of system charges, central generation does pay for using transmission (roughly EUR1.6 per MWh).

■ Some small plants are still captive customers and so sell their output directly to the local distributor, who is obliged to buy it.

---

49. *Cogen Europe, 1999.*

■ Although large distributed generation is generally paying full costs for connection and use of system, and the rules about this were initially too rigid, most industrial CHP producers are now satisfied that more flexible rules are being worked out.

■ Rules regarding imbalance charges have been adjusted to help DG. The Dutch introduced their new electricity trading arrangements in January 2001. These arrangements penalised power producers that could not predict their output accurately (two hours in advance of delivery) through imbalance charges. Wind producers were particularly disadvantaged because of the difficulties in forecasting wind speeds within that time period. Initially, imbalance charges and volumes were high and caused some hardship. However, this situation led to a review by the system operator, which decided to allow producers to make final adjustments to their predicted output only one hour in advance, effective at the end of March 2001[50].

Market liberalisation has had a number of interesting effects on the market for distributed generation, particularly CHP[51]:

■ Electricity prices have generally fallen as a result of overcapacity in the Netherlands and due to lower prices from imported electricity in neighbouring countries with excess capacity.

■ CHP plants, which formerly received favourable natural gas tariffs, now purchase natural gas competitively.

■ Rises in natural gas prices have financially strained CHP plants. Plants with large power-generation components have been more strongly affected. One went bankrupt.

As a result of the financial difficulties faced by the CHP units, the government responded in late 2000 with measures to support CHP further, including:

■ An increase in the Energy Investment Allowance (a tax credit) for new CHP.

---

50. DTE, 2001.
51. See ECN, 2000.

■ Exemption of CHP electricity consumption from the regulatory energy tax.

■ Financial support to CHP output up to 200 GWh of EUR2.28 per MWh.

These measures supplemented an accelerated depreciation program (known as VAMIL) for CHP investments that met certain efficiency targets.

In 2001, new rules were proposed to increase financial support for CHP output to EUR5.7 per MWh to a maximum of 1 000 GWh per plant, provided that the unit meets certain efficiency targets.

As a result of the financial strain on CHP, the government is under pressure to alter network tariffs, for example, to waive connection fees for large CHP. The government is reluctant to use the network as a mechanism for subsidising generation. However, distribution companies are examining different tariff proposals to reward CHP that adds value to the local grid, such as in the form of voltage or reactive power.

Despite the current financial difficulties with CHP, new large CHP projects continue to be announced. Much of this capacity will, however, be connected at high voltage.

The United Kingdom

Electricity markets in most of the United Kingdom have been fully liberalised since 1999, as have natural gas markets. Electricity laws and regulations require distribution network operators (DNOs) to be legally separate from electricity generation or retailing businesses. The Utilities Act 2000 also specifies that the DNOs have a duty to promote competition in electricity.

Much recent policy development on distributed generation (known as "embedded generation" and which includes wind power in the UK) has focused on its environmental benefit, particularly regarding climate change. As a consequence, in addition to measures to support renewable energy, the government has developed several to promote CHP:

■ A target to raise CHP capacity from 4.6 GW in 2000 to 10 GW in 2010.

■ An exemption from the climate-change levy on fuel for "good quality CHP".

■ Exemption of CHP from business taxes.

■ An 80% discount on their climate-change levy for industries installing CHP, in agreements between particular industries and the government on climate-change measures.

■ Support for the modernisation of community-heating systems.

Partly as a result of these measures, "good quality" CHP capacity has grown by 1.3 GW a year in the past four years. Nearly half of the total of 4.6 GW was added in 2000. The total additional capacity generated 23.3 TWh of electricity at an average capacity factor of 57% and overall efficiency of 71%. CHP power generation accounts for approximately 6% of total electricity generated in the UK. These figures exclude 5.4 GW of CHP plant that did not meet the "good quality" criteria[52].

---

52. *"Good Quality" CHP is defined as achieving a certain minimum efficiency of heat and electricity production from the CHP project. The required power efficiency is at least 20% (15% until 2005 for existing projects), with a required combined heat and power efficiency that decreases as power output increases. For a small CHP scheme (1-10 MW) producing power at 20% efficiency, the required CHP efficiency would be 69%. See CHPQA 2000 and Annex I of this report.*

In addition to these measures to promote CHP and renewable energy, the government has identified the development of embedded generation in general as important to increase competition among electricity producers.

Market liberalisation has also meant that charges for using the grid have been unbundled, so that distributors generators need only pay for the grid services they use. As in the Netherlands, power from distributed producers is exempt from charges from the use of transmission system and associated losses, and requirements for balancing. This exemption results in a competitive advantage for DG, compared with centrally generated power, of USD3-USD4 per MWh.

The creation of the New Electricity Trading Arrangements (NETA) was part of the government's efforts to enhance competition in the electricity sector. However, embedded generators were concerned that NETA, which became operational in March 2001, would work to their disadvantage. NETA abolished the system whereby embedded generators could effectively supply the local network and receive wholesale prices, regardless of the costs of balancing their output. Instead, NETA required all generators to predict their output at least 3.5 hours in advance; they pay penalties if they produce less than forecast but receive only modest compensation if they produce more. These rules were designed to give all producers incentives to balance their outputs, but wind producers (because their output is difficult to predict) and some CHP producers felt that the new rules would be burdensome for embedded generators.

Ofgem published an assessment of the effect of NETA on small generators. The report, published a few months after the implementation of the arrangements, showed that they hurt small generators, though principally through a decline in power prices[53]. Specifically, Ofgem found that:

■ Electricity prices received by small generators fell by around 17%, somewhat less than the price decline in the overall wholesale market. Prices for CHP fell around 12%.

---

53. Ofgem, 2001a.

- Costs to generators rose by 16%, mostly due to fuel costs.

- Overall exports by small generators fell 44%. The drop for CHP was over 60%.

- While smaller generators were concerned about predicting their output accurately, with the exception of wind generators, their actual imbalances were not much greater than for larger plants.

- The balancing mechanism sends a strong signal to avoid imbalances. A generator supplying more power than committed output netted only USD13 per MWh from June to July 2001. Producing less than the committed output cost USD58 per MWh. This compares to an average selling price of USD34 per MWh.

On the other hand, the Ofgem report clearly shows that the new trading arrangements can create additional costs for distributed generators since:

- Participation in the market as a generator or supplier, or both, involves large transaction costs. Many DG producers, which are relatively small, cannot afford such costs. Thus, they are discouraged from participating directly in the market and are encouraged to work with a larger supplier.

- For all generators, imbalance comes at a price, but most existing DG systems cannot completely control balances. Most of them are either genuinely variable generators (such as wind) or CHP. Their power sales to the system are dictated by customer load and heat requirements.

The report also found that the separation of distribution from the sale of electricity removed any incentive for the former distribution utility (now a "Distribution Network Operator" or DNO) to encourage local generation.

To further investigate the implications of NETA for DG systems, in early 2000 the government formed the Embedded Generation Working Group (EGWG), comprising distributed generators and other stakeholders. The EGWG studied:

- The role of the DNO in facilitating competition in generation.

■ The contribution of DG to network performance and security.

■ Charging principles for both connection and use of the distribution network.

■ The role of "micro" DG.

■ The impact of DG on design and evolution of distribution network.

The central problem identified in the EGWG report, published in January 2001, is the lack of incentives for DNOs to encourage DG development[54]. On the contrary, DNOs find DG to be an additional cost and distraction from their main business of delivering electricity to consumers. As a consequence, DG developers face several barriers. First, they have little information about where to make an economical connection in the distribution network. Each DNO has its own procedures for applying for connection. DNOs either aren't interested or don't invest in active generator or load management technologies. Since DNOs are regulated monopolies, the role of the regulator (Ofgem) is critical in changing the situation. The underlying message is that Ofgem will need to give DNOs an incentive to take a more active role in managing their networks in real time, much like transmission network operators.

A second key issue is the level of charges for both connection and operation. Currently, DG pays "deep" connection charges, i.e. it pays for not only the cost of connecting to the nearest network supply point, but also for network reinforcement at higher voltages. While these deep charges give DG a locational price signal, they can raise project costs. The report proposes various compromise arrangements where the reinforcement costs are shared between the network operator (and ultimately other consumers) and the DG developer.

A third issue explored in the report regards the role of household DG, mainly micro-CHP. The main barrier is the need for the simpler connection requirement (which applies only to PV installations) to be extended, where practical, to micro-CHP.

---

54. DTI, 2001a.

Finally, DNOs were found to have little information about the potential value of DG in deferring expansion of distribution networks or in providing ancillary services. The report recognises that if DG is to play a big role in the expansion of generating capacity, DNOs must be able to give developers estimates of the benefits of DG for the network.

Most of the report's specific recommendations are directed at Ofgem, which as the network regulator is responsible for developing the detailed regulatory policies to address the government's objectives.

DTI and Ofgem are jointly chairing a group to implement the EGWG recommendations. Ofgem has identified the following priorities:

■ Amending the overall regulatory framework to facilitate competition in generation and ensure that embedded generators aren't discriminated against.

■ Analysing the implications of growth in embedded generation.

■ Making changes to price-control mechanisms.

■ Analysing the implications of micro-generation for network operation.

In September 2001, Ofgem issued a consultation paper on price controls and incentives for DNOs regarding embedded generation that proposes[55]:

■ Encouraging DNOs to introduce shallow connection charges and to allow them to recover other costs through use-of-system charges.

■ Requiring DNOs to publish the basis for connection charges and charges for the use of the distribution system by embedded generators.

■ Requiring simple, standard connection procedures and charges for microgeneration (i.e. household generation).

■ Requiring separate meters for electricity imported to and exported from the embedded generator's site.

---

55. *Ofgem, 2001b.*

■ Making additional technical information available to prospective generators regarding network development needs.

A Distributed Generation Co-ordinating Group has now been established to follow up on the recommendations of the Embedded Generation Working Group[56]. In addition, the UK government has proposed measures to: ensure that imbalance prices genuinely reflect costs, develop new mechanisms to encourage smaller generators to consolidate, and examine changes to NETA rules that affect smaller generators[57].

Summary

Each of the four countries considered in this chapter has their own policy issues arising from their specific circumstances. Table 8 summarises these issues and circumstances in terms of share of distributed-generation capacity, the sectors involved in market reform, and the numbers and types of distribution companies.

---

56. *DTI, 2001b.*
57. *DTI, 2001c.*

Table 8

Comparison of Distributed-Generation Issues in Japan, the US, the Netherlands, and the UK

DG Capacity	Status of Market Share (%)	Distribution Liberalisation	Key DG Companies	Issues
Japan	3	Large customers only	10 vertically integrated utilities (VIUs)	Grid access Competition vs. utilities
The United States	6	Varies by state (0-100%)	200 + VIUs, 2 900 + municipal/rural distributors	Interconnection standards Environmental standards Market access Backup power charges
The Netherlands	30	Large and medium	20 municipal/regional distributors	CHP finances Climate change Grid benefits
The United Kingdom	6	All customers	12 distributors	CHP finances New market rules Grid benefits Micro-CHP

POLICY ISSUES

This chapter assesses the policy issues raised in the last chapter that arise from distributed generation. These issues can be grouped under the three Es of energy policy: economic efficiency, environmental protection, and energy security. Under the heading of economic efficiency, issues include:

■ market access, i.e. the connection of distributed generation to distribution grids and to distribution networks;

■ pricing, i.e. incorporating the benefits and costs of distributed power in distribution network tariffs; and

■ market conditions. In the area of environment, the report considers emissions and the effect of regulations on DG technologies.

As for energy security, the report examines the implications of distributed generation for the diversification of fuels and reliability of the electricity sector.

Economic Efficiency

■ Grid Interconnection

Distribution networks traditionally have been designed to take power from high voltage grids and distribute this power to end consumers. The introduction of generating capacity connected to the distribution system need not cause great changes to this system, provided that the capacity does not actually send power into the network.

Once power is sent into the network, the flows of electricity will be changed and even reversed from the normal design. This can lead to a number of technical problems that can affect the stability of the network and quality of electricity supplied. These problems include[58]:

■ **Voltage control.** Distribution network operators are normally obliged to keep network voltages within a certain range. Electricity sent into the distribution network tends to cause an increase in voltage. This can be beneficial in some instances (e.g. for some rural

---

58. For a detailed discussion, see Jenkins N., R. Allan, P. Crossley, D. Kirschen and G. Strbac, 2000.

networks) where operators have problems with low voltages. But in a system operating under normal conditions, these electricity flows can cause difficulties. Difficulties can be alleviated by requiring connection at higher voltage or by upgrading transformers for improved local voltage control. There are related concerns with voltage fluctuations and their potential impact on neighbouring consumers.

■ **Reactive power.** Depending on the type of generation, DG can either supply reactive power or will be dependent on it.

■ **Protection.** DG flows can reduce the effectiveness of protection equipment and create operational difficulties under certain conditions. For example, while customers may want the ability to operate in "island" mode (separate from the grid) during a distribution circuit outage, restoring power to them involves important technical and safety considerations. Protection systems are required to ensure that DG systems are not supplying the network during outage conditions and can be resynchronised to the grid when power is restored.

Interconnection of distributed generation may appear to be a purely technical issue but a number of policy concerns are involved. The lack of technical interconnection standards in the US, for example, has led a proliferation of requirements. Second, the ability of distributors to deal with distributed generation varies according to utility size and experience. Finally, regardless of expertise, a utility may see distributed generation as a competitor and may impede interconnection. This is particularly a concern for a non-liberalised system or non-liberalised consumers, and where vertically integrated utilities can use interconnection requirements (or prices for backup services) to discourage distributed generation.

The development of interconnection standards, guidelines for dealing with interconnection requests, and procedures to help distributors assess the effect of distributed generation on a local distribution system will reduce transaction costs (the full costs of interconnection) for distributors and developers. The use of national standards is common in Europe; these are usually stricter than the European norm (EN 50160). The US is currently considering protection standards (IEEE standard P1547) that would reduce guesswork by utilities and DG developers about the kinds of protection equipment that are needed.

Finally, for household generation such as household PV or micro-CHP, connection costs could be a big percentage of the cost of the system, if it must adhere to technical standards developed for large generation. If there are only a few domestic systems, technical protection requirements can be simplified. Obviously, the more such systems there are, the more complex the requirements would have to be.

■ Electricity Market Reform and Distributed Generation

Prior to electricity market reform, distributed generation in OECD countries was carried out under a controlled situation. For generators not exporting to the grid, distributed generation simply displaced power purchased from the grid. For DG exporting into the grid, the output was usually purchased by the vertically integrated utility, normally under a long-term contract. The main policy issues associated with DG at this stage were the prices charged for backup power for ancillary services, and the prices paid for exported electricity.

Market liberalisation has affected distributed generation by:

■ Increasing market opportunities by opening access to networks.

■ Increasing market complexity.

■ Placing a premium on the flexibility of a technology or system.

■ Freeing the prices of electricity and natural gas.

Market liberalisation opens access to the distribution network, thus giving distributed generators the opportunity to sell their power directly to customers. Distributed generators, therefore, have the potential to increase competition in the supply of electricity and thereby support economic efficiency.

Market liberalisation has greatly increased the complexity of the structure of the market, its operation, and pricing for all power producers, including distributed generators. Wholesale markets have been created, pricing has become more dynamic, and the geographic scope of markets has broadened.

While these changes have had consequences for all generators, distributed generators have been more strongly affected due to their smaller size and proportionately higher costs of dealing with:

■ **Competition.** Existing distributed generators are now competing in a geographically larger market, where generation capacity may be held by a few, big owners.

■ **Bilateral contracts.** Generators are encouraged to enter into bilateral contracts with consumers to reduce exposure to volatile prices in spot electricity markets.

■ **Scheduled energy dispatch.** Electricity-trading arrangements have been introduced that require generators to declare the amount of energy they export to the grid. While inability to meet this commitment results in penalties, excess generation has low rewards.

■ **Procurement of backup power.** Distributed generators must now purchase backup power in case of equipment failure, instead of receiving it at regulated rates from the distributor.

The liberalisation of electricity markets has also changed the way power-generation technologies are valued. Attributes such as short construction lead times, low capital costs, flexibility in operation, and ability to expand output are likely to be more greatly valued. Distributed technologies that have these attributes can expect to benefit.

While the reforms have greatly increased the complexity of doing business, the indirect short-term effects have been even more profound. Electricity prices have *fallen* in Western Europe as a result of excess capacity and the increased geographic scope for trading electricity. Electricity prices are also falling in Japan. This has been coupled with large increases in natural gas prices.

As a result, generators in Western Europe are under financial strain. Those dependent on gas-fired generation and the CHP industry, which principally use natural gas for power generation, have been particularly affected. Some CHP producers have depended on revenue from electricity sales to ensure profitability. However, many of them considered these sales to be a side business. They made fewer efforts to reduce financial risk in this area than in their main business.

Some CHP producers have responded to market conditions by cutting back on output or stopping CHP altogether. A few have gone bankrupt. On the other hand, CHP facilities that have been more "balanced" with respect to heat and power generation, i.e. less reliant on revenue from electricity sales, have been less financially affected. The rise in prices for natural gas has given new CHP an incentive to make more efficient use of that resource.

Despite the temporary negative effects of market liberalisation on CHP, governments have responded with concern about the need for policies to expand CHP, particularly programmes to provide financial relief. The Dutch government recently agreed to provide an incentive of EUR5.7 per MWh to CHP producers for 2001. The German government has gone further and recently passed a subsidy system for CHP electricity that will offer subsidies to existing CHP until the year 2010. The cost of the German programme, estimated at EUR4.09 billion, is to be recovered from consumer tariffs.

On the whole, market liberalisation is exposing all power producers to financial risks of the marketplace. DG producers, like the others, have to be able to respond. In the long run, current conditions may encourage new DG development to be more efficient and lower cost.

Regarding the inclusion of DG in the liberalised electricity market, there are, however, important issues to consider in the areas of market structure, market operation, and pricing. These are discussed in the following sections.

■ Market Structure

Liberalisation of the retail market is vital for the economically efficient development of distributed generation. Retail liberalisation involves access by producers and customers to the distribution system. With DG as an option, customers can generate their own power in response to signals from the market.

If the reforms are limited to wholesale liberalisation, the distributed generator essentially faces the same conditions as under the monopoly regime. This might well be favourable to DG if there are obligations for its purchase. In that case, however, the DG is unlikely to be economically efficient. For example, excess capacity in the Dutch market can at least partly be attributed to policies that encouraged the creation of decentralised generation regardless of need.

Limited reforms might also be unfavourable to distributed generation. In some markets, only high-voltage consumers have the ability to choose suppliers. Smaller customers must notify the vertically integrated utility of their intent to install distributed generation. The utility can respond by offering to discount the regulated electricity price in order to discourage the installation of DG.

Thus, while the liberalisation of the retail market may be a necessary condition for development, it is not a sufficient condition to ensure that DG receives nondiscriminatory access. Distribution companies that continue to own generating capacity to supply their customers directly will still have an incentive to discriminate against distributed generation. Separation of distribution from generation and retail remove this incentive to discriminate.

The inability of distributors to own and operate DG, however, may result in some inefficiency. For example, the operation of distributed generation at a transformer station to relieve distribution-system congestion is forbidden under the conditions of separation but may be the most efficient solution.

■ Market Operation

Electricity trading is a central feature of liberalised electricity systems. In most OECD countries with liberalised markets, spot markets exist for the trade of wholesale electricity. Although spot electricity markets may furnish a small share of final customer demand, they play an important role in setting prices and in fine-tuning the balance between supply and demand.

Not surprisingly, electricity-trading systems are organised to serve participants at the transmission level. However, the markets are not run entirely to the disadvantage of distributed generators. They offer them a number of advantages:

■ A framework for accessing other market participants, customers, genera-tors, aggregators (and others) and for entering into supply agreements.

■ A potential market for ancillary services[59].

■ Transmission-price unbundling, which in some markets requires central generators (not DG) to pay some transmission costs.

■ An ability to choose suppliers of backup power.

■ An ability to aggregate supply from a number of sites.

The New Electricity Trading Arrangements (NETA) in the UK clearly show how the generator can capture the benefits of distributed generation. The UK regulator, Ofgem, has estimated the "embedded benefit", essentially the charges central generators pay that embedded generators need not pay, as shown in Table 9.

Table 9

Estimates of "Embedded Benefit" to Distributed Generators in the UK (in USD per MWh)

Embedded Benefit	London	South Yorkshire	North
Transmission Network Use of System charges avoided (Demand)	2.73	0.99	0.20
Transmission Network Use of System charges avoided (Generation)	− 2.10	0.75	1.73
Balancing System Use of System charges avoided	1.77	1.77	1.77
Transmission Losses charges avoided	0.06	0.06	0.06
Balancing system administrative costs avoided	0.29	0.29	0.29
Avoided trading charges	0.06	0.06	0.06
Total	2.80	3.92	4.10

Source: Ofgem.

---

59. Currently in the UK, ancillary service operations are co-ordinated centrally by the transmission system operator (TSO). In practise, there is a size limit below which certain ancillary services can be reliably monitored and co-ordinated by the TSO. While there is significant experience in contracting for reserve and frequency response, high unit costs for monitoring, metering, and communication limit the economic effectiveness of DG participating in these markets. Aggregation of smaller DG might increase the possibilities (see Kirby, B. and E. Hirst, 2001).

The transmission-charging system in the UK is designed to provide incentives for *central* generation in areas where load exceeds generation (as in London) and disincentives where generation exceeds load (as in the North). However, since it doesn't pay location-based charges, distributed generation has less "embedded benefit" to locate in London and greater incentive to locate in the north of England. When transmission pricing does not vary by location (so-called "postage-stamp"), there is no incentive to locate new generating capacity to relieve congestion.

Market liberalisation has created other costs for distributed generators, some of which are related to size. Participation in the market as a generator or supplier (or both as the case may be for DG), involves large transaction costs. Many DG producers, which are relatively small, cannot afford such costs. Thus, they are discouraged from participating directly in the market and are encouraged to work with a larger supplier.

The trend toward requiring generators and loads to balance their requirements may particularly affect DG. The Dutch electricity trading arrangements begun in January 2001 and the New Electricity Trading Arrangements (NETA) in the UK effective as of March 2001 require generators supplying power to the grid and retail suppliers taking power from the grid to meet their forecasted output or to pay penalties for any shortfall. As an immediate result, balancing markets were created in both countries, where producers pay high prices for their imbalances. Distributed generators were particularly affected by these changes because of their relatively small size and difficulty in balancing their output.

In the Dutch market, a rule was changed that reduced the final commitment time for generators to one hour from two. As a result, imbalances have declined substantially[60].

In the UK market, small generator output to the grid has dropped by 44% since the introduction of NETA. The dramatic decrease may well be the primary result of market conditions, namely, the fall in electricity prices

---

60. *Problems with very small CHP units in the Netherlands are avoided because they are owned by "captive" customers. Distributors are obliged to buy their output regardless of balancing.*

and the rise in fuel costs. However, the balancing mechanism also appears to be a factor for plants that have difficulty predicting their output.

Distributed generators in the UK have complained that the new imbalance mechanism is discouraging new CHP and renewables, contrary to the government's policy. However, the imbalance mechanism does reflect a real cost to the electricity system: units with variable output will create a need for a system operator to carry a larger primary reserve. Early evidence from the NETA suggests that small generators (at least those still exporting) are coping better than expected with the mechanism. They have not been much more variable in their output than large generators. If some of the other benefits of DG technologies – such as reducing distribution congestion or providing ancillary services – are to be realised, the electricity system must be able to schedule supply to the network.

For wind in the UK market, the variability of power output is 40%-50%, very high compared with roughly 5% or less for large generators. Better weather-forecasting software is becoming available that claims to be able to reduce the variability between forecast and actual output to 5%-8%[61].

Other simple steps could reduce considerably the exposure of distributed generation to imbalance markets. With shorter commitment times for output (as in the Netherlands), DG can more easily make better forecasts and thus reduce their imbalances. Mechanisms to encourage smaller DG producers to work together would help them to reduce their net imbalances and the resulting imbalance charges, and enable them to take advantage of economies of scale. Finally, very small producers such as household PV should be treated like variations in household loads.

■ Pricing

Prices are the key signal for influencing market behaviour. Prices are supposed to reflect underlying demand and supply conditions at different locations and at different times within the electricity system. The trend in liberalised markets is toward increasingly exposing customers and generators to the variability of electricity prices.

---

61. See Zacharias, P. and K. Rohrig, 2001.

Such pricing trends will, at least in principle, encourage the more economically efficient development of all generation, including distributed generation. Whenever there is a surplus of generating capacity in the system, prices will be low, discouraging the construction of new power generation and the use of higher cost existing generation. Conversely, when demand is tight, price increases price should encourage new capacity.

Distributed generation should benefit from such pricing reform. Customer exposure to the higher costs of electricity during peak periods encourages the development of distributed generation. Time-of-use rates in Japan are credited with the installation of cogeneration systems that operate only during peak hours. Distributed generation, by reducing purchases from the network, is also seen as a mechanism for reducing customer exposure to the volatility of electricity prices.

■ Pricing and Location

From the point of view of the electricity network, however, distributed generation offers maximum economic efficiency gains because of its flexibility in location. A distributed generator brings value to a distribution system insofar as its location defers expansion of distribution assets, reduces distribution-system losses, or delivers network support or ancillary services.

Location-based pricing for distributed generation falls into three categories:

■ **Connection charges.** Charges for connection to the grid can include the full costs of connection, including location-dependent system upgrades.

■ **Operating charges.** Charges for services provided to the local network, e.g. to relieve congestion, to provide voltage support, to pay for the costs of serving DG, and to reduce losses.

■ **Congestion-related pricing.** Tariffs paid by all load customers for distribution services that rise or fall according to the level of congestion.

Connection charges, the most common type of location-based pricing, can be a large barrier to distributed generation. Some operating charges are an incentive to DG, particularly those aimed at reducing distribution losses, as they are already reflected in system prices. Congestion-related pricing is not carried out at the retail level. However, in some systems distributed generators can be rewarded for deferral of upgrades to the distribution system.

■ Connection Charges

In the UK, DG developers pay the full cost of connection, known as "deep" connection charges, up front. This approach factors in location-based prices and in principle allows for discounts to these charges for the value of generation deferral. Partially as a consequence, DG does not pay any charge for use of the distribution system but also does not receive any additional charges or credits from the distributor for losses or ancillary services.

By contrast, in the Netherlands, DG pays only the direct or "shallow" connection costs for distribution. Distributed generators larger than 10 MVA also pay costs for using the system. However, these use-of-system charges are not location-dependent. At the urging of the government, distributors in the Netherlands are currently developing a tariff proposal that would reward DG for contributions to the system (e.g. in reducing losses).

There are advantages to both systems. The UK system sends a stronger "locational" signal but can be a barrier for DG, as connection costs can amount to a large percentage of installation costs. Furthermore, an upgrade usually allows more than one DG on the system. Subsequent DG may not need to pay and can "free ride", arguably distorting competition with the first-comer[62]. The Dutch system, while encouraging DG entry, presents the opposite problem.

---

62. The French system is a hybrid of the UK system. It has deep connection charges but allows a DG to collect revenues from subsequent DG installations that benefit from the upgrade.

The lack of a locational price signal can lead to overinvestment that has to be recovered from all customers, not just those benefiting from DG[63].

The position of distributed generators stands in contrast with that of high-voltage "central" generators. Central generators typically do not pay "deep" costs for connection, even though one or more of them may require a major upgrade to the transmission network. Increasingly, however, transmission system charges are including locational signals to encourage generators to locate closer to loads.

In both the UK and the Netherlands, distribution systems are obliged to provide non-discriminatory access to generators and to consumers. In addition, in the UK, the Utilities Act gives distributors a duty to promote competition. In both countries, distribution-network operators tend to be neutral overall and indifferent about offering locational information that would assist developers in choosing sites for distributed generation.

A compromise between "deep" or "shallow" approaches that encompasses the efficiency of location-based connection pricing and "competitive neutrality" (non-discrimination between central and distributed generation, and greater competition among participants) might consist of the following:

■ Distributors provide detailed information about distribution capacity and identify areas of congestion, to accommodate DG at various points in the network.

■ New DG pays "shallow" connection charges up front.

■ Additional expenditures by the distributor to accommodate a DG project are recovered from both DG and all loads though system charges. The share attributed to the DG project is reduced if more DG is connected that can use the upgrade.

---

63. *The small size of the Netherlands is, of course, a factor in the decision to use postage-stamp pricing.*

■ Operating Charges

Distributed generation will reduce system losses by reducing the total amount of electricity delivered through the distribution system. Customers with DG already capture this benefit to some extent, as losses are reflected in distribution charges. However, these charges typically do not distinguish differences in losses by location. Generally speaking, losses are much higher in rural networks than in urban areas. (See Table 10). If charges for losses differ by location, distribution customers, especially those receiving power at low voltage, will have a greater incentive to generate their own electricity.

Table 10

New South Wales (Australia) Distribution Loss factors

Customer voltage	Loss factor – urban	Loss factor – rural
132/110 kV	1.0047	1.013
33 kV	1.0124	1.052
11 kV bus	1.0156	1.057
11 kV line	1.0277	1.1
LV bus	1.0398	1.153
LV line	1.0752	1.188

Source: NEMMCO

Furthermore, on any given transmission or distribution line, losses vary as the square of the current the line carries. Since losses during peak hours are greater, the value of DG operating during peak hours is correspondingly larger.

It is more difficult to assess the effect on losses of DG power exported into the distribution system. Urban DG, as it is adjacent to other loads, may be more effective at reducing losses.

Regulations can be developed that reward distributors for reducing losses that might, as a result, encourage DG with a good location. DG reduces deliveries of electricity, however, which in turn can lessen a distributor's revenues.

In some locations, DG can be helpful in furnishing voltage support. Regulatory incentives to improve the quality of electricity supply can encourage distributors to reward DG for this service.

■ Congestion Pricing

The way to efficiently relieve distribution congestion is obvious, in principle: All load customers would pay a congestion-dependent tariff for distribution services. Customers in a congested system are encouraged to reduce their demand, either through a demand-side measure or through the installation of their own generation. Power exported into the distribution system from customers that reduce congestion would be rewarded by higher prices. Such a pricing system would provide the right incentives to DG.

Such a system may be difficult to put into practice. There has been great reluctance to expose electricity consumers to congestion charges, even at the transmission level, for equity reasons. Furthermore, it remains to be proven whether the systemic benefits from congestion-based prices exceed the costs.

Without such a pricing system, the distribution-system operator remains the key entity in managing congestion on the system and attempting to do so at least cost. The distributor, given regulatory incentives to carry out this task, will find it profitable to pay a customer to supply electricity (or reduce demand) during congested periods. While upgrades to the distribution system can be made more quickly (1-3 years) compared with transmission upgrades, so can upgrades to DG systems, particularly at a site already containing DG.

■ Net Metering

In developing policies to promote some distributed technologies, there is a temptation to modify the design or operation of the electricity market to increase the penetration of DG technologies. Net metering, which pays small generators retail electricity prices for power supplied to the local grid, is an example of a support policy sometimes offered to household customers producing power with PV.

Such approaches forgo economic efficiency and can distort markets. In a fully liberalised electricity market, small generators – whether PV or micro-CHP – should be able to choose their retailers or consumers. The local distributor, depending on the market design, then may no longer be in the business of purchasing electricity for sale to consumers but instead of raising revenue on the amount of electricity delivered.

The Embedded Generation Working Group in the UK identified a number of problems with net metering, such as the effect on distributor revenues, and examined ten different metering and charging options[64]. The report concludes that the issue of net energy tariffs is complex and needs a detailed cost-benefit analysis.

Price signals are a logical way to encourage DG developers to locate their plant efficiently and discourage them from locating where they would place additional costs on the system. Deep connection charges, as in the UK, are an example of such pricing.

However, such prices must also consider other factors besides economic efficiency gains. Competitive neutrality may be impaired if efficient pricing rules are applied to DG and not central generators. There is an inequality, for example, if distributed generators are liable for all of the costs of upgrades to the distribution network incurred by their connection but if generators connecting at high voltage are not. Furthermore, the costs and complexity of putting into place an ideal location-based pricing may exceed the benefits. Finally, the social equity aspects of pricing must also be considered. Location-based pricing, in particular, is likely to result in higher tariffs for rural consumers.

Environmental Protection

Distributed generation embraces a wide range of technologies with a wide range of emissions. For fossil-fired distributed technologies, there are two key areas of concern: NO_x emissions on local and regional air quality, and greenhouse-gas emissions on climate change.

---

64. *EGWG Report, Annex 5, "Options for Domestic and Other Micro-Scale Generation".*

■ Air Quality

Figure 6 summarises the NO$_x$ emissions from different technologies in kg per MWh generated. The first point to note is that NO$_x$ emissions among DG technologies vary by a factor of 2 000 from fuel cells (at the low end) to diesel power (at the top) partly due to differences in design (for fuel cells) and partly because of the large reductions in emissions that can be achieved from emissions-control technologies. Emissions control by Selective Catalytic Reduction (SCR) increases in cost per kW as size decreases. It is prohibitively expensive for a smaller plant.

Figure 6

NO$_x$ Emissions from Distributed-Generation Technologies (kg/MWh)

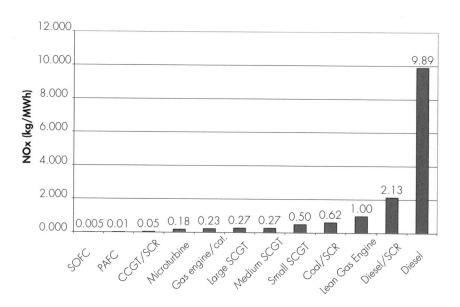

Notes: SCGT = simple cycle gas turbine, SOFC = Solid Oxide Fuel Cell, PAFC = Phosphoric Acid Fuel Cell, Lean Gas engine = lean fuel mixture gas engine, Gas engine/cat. = Gas engine with three-way catalyst, /SCR = with selective catalyst (NO$_x$) reduction technology, Source: RAP 2001 (www.rapmaine.org), except Coal/SCR from new US EPA Standard (0.15 lb./mmBTU) assuming net efficiency of 37% (including transmission and distribution losses). Assumed CCGT efficiency of 51% includes transmission and distribution losses.

Diesel stands out as a high NO_x-emitting technology. Even when fitted with selective catalytic reduction (SCR) emissions control, its emissions are higher than for a similarly equipped central coal-fired station.

In general, for electricity systems with a large share of coal-fired electricity and with advanced NO_x control, NO_x emissions will be much higher than for a gas engine. In these cases, the installation of gas-fired DG can reduce NO_x emissions. Gas engines require some form of emissions control (such as three-way catalysts similar to those on cars) to bring their emissions below those of a coal plant with SCR control.

Except for fuel cells, none of the fossil-distributed technologies can match the NO_x performance of a combined-cycle gas turbine equipped with SCR control, even when operating as a CHP plant[65].

The emissions of NO_x from distributed generation are attracting increased environmental regulatory attention. In Japan, national emissions standards for diesel engines are high enough to permit their installation. In larger cities, stricter limits apply that effectively eliminate diesels from consideration (see Table 11).

Table 11

Japanese NO_x limits on Cogeneration Systems

	National NO_x limit (ppm at 0% O_2[66])	Tokyo NO_x limit (ppm)
Gas Turbine	294	100
Diesel Engine	2 493	300
Gas Engine	600	200

Source: Japan CGC, 2001.

---

65. See Kaarsberg, T. J. Bluestein, J. Romm, and A. Rosenfeld, 1998.

66. For comparison with ppm at 15% O_2, multiply by 0.28. Thus, the regulated level for gas turbines in Tokyo corresponds to 28 ppmv at 15% O_2. This compares with the California figure for turbines of 0.23 kg per kWh output which is based on 9 ppmv at 15% O_2.

In the United States, limits are generally set on a local or regional basis. Recent rulings in some high-emission areas have set a standard based on the combined-cycle gas turbine with SCR control (see Table 12).

Table 12

Examples of NO_x Limits in the US Applicable to Distributed Generation (in kg/MWh)

	West Texas	East Texas	California
Gas Turbine	1.4	0.21 (0.06 beginning in 2005)	0.09 (12-50 MW) 0.23 (< 3 MW)
Gas/Diesel Engine	1.4	As above	0.1
Central plant	0.06 for all plants greater than 10 MW	0.06 for all plants greater than 10 MW	0.02

Sources: TNRCC, 2001. CARB, 2001.

The standards for East Texas applicable as of 2005 would permit a large combined-cycle power station equipped with selective catalytic reduction but not small, gas-fired DG because of a higher specific emissions rate. The California standard does show sensitivity to size. Both Texas and California, in estimating emissions, use output-based standards that give full credit to the useful energy output of a CHP plant.

■ Greenhouse-Gas Emissions

Carbon-dioxide emissions from fossil DG technologies are shown in Figure 7.

Figure 7

CO_2 Emissions from Distributed-Generation Technologies (in kg/MWh)

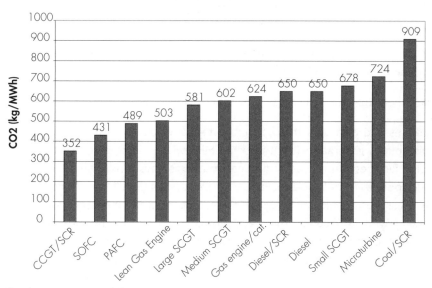

Notes/sources: same as previous figure.

The figure shows that all fossil-fired DG technologies that operate without heat recovery have higher carbon-dioxide emissions[67] than the combined-cycle plant and somewhat lower emissions than the coal plant. Therefore, increased use of fossil DG will result in a reduction in

---

67. *Fuel-cell emission rates come from use of natural gas as the source of hydrogen.*

greenhouse-gas emissions, if the DG is displacing coal-fired electricity or if the DG is a CHP system.

Assessing the greenhouse-gas emissions from CHP is complex. The complexity arises from assumptions about what type of electricity and heat production the CHP unit is replacing. A UK study estimated that domestic CHP with an overall efficiency of 67% (19% electricity) reduced CO_2 emissions by 41% in 1999, assuming that it displaced the current mix of generating capacity and boilers. However, the savings are 20% assuming that the CHP displaces only new gas-fired generation and gas-fired boilers[68]. Calculating emissions savings from CHP is explained in detail in Annex I.

With improvements in central station efficiency (with new gas-turbine plants claiming efficiencies of up to 56%[69]), CHP schemes will reduce greenhouse gas emissions, provided that:

■ They use low (or no carbon fuels) such as natural gas, renewables, or waste fuels (e.g. refinery gas).

■ When they use natural gas, they achieve a high overall efficiency.

Policies and measures that encourage higher efficiency in the use of distributed generation (e.g. through CHP) or upgrading of outdated CHP facilities can reduce total greenhouse gas emissions. One set of such policies is the "good quality CHP" measures in the UK (see Annex I). Measures should be designed so that distributed generators are encouraged to reduce their emissions. In particular, the use of economic instruments (such as carbon-emissions trading) would encourage DG operators to design and operate their facilities to minimise emissions of greenhouse gases.

Energy Security

The implications of distributed power for energy security take two forms: first, on the diversification of primary energy supplies and second, on the reliability of electricity supply.

---

68. DTI, 2000.
69. 60% before accounting for transmission and distribution losses.

■ Energy Diversification

The impact on primary fuels depends on the technology used in distributed generation. The use of photovoltaic systems results in diversification of supply away from fossil fuels. Most of the other technologies rely directly or indirectly (in the case of fuel cells) on natural gas. Given that much of the new investment in generating technology is directed toward natural gas, the effect of distributed generation on supply diversity is limited. CHP is seen to contribute to energy security because its higher fuel efficiency results in lower overall fuel consumption.

Japan is a possible exception, since much of its DG capacity is oil-fired. Enlarging DG capacity will, in principle, increase Japan's dependence on oil. Less than 2% of all power generation is currently DG, however, so the impact on energy security currently is very limited.

■ Electricity-System Reliability

The reliability of the electricity system can be enhanced by distributed generation. The availability of standby generators in tight US electricity markets in the summer of 2001 helped reduce the risk of blackouts. Better integration of standby resources into system operations can further enhance the electricity system's security of supply. Furthermore, the use of distributed generators at selected locations helps distributors overcome local bottlenecks in the distribution system. Increased distributed generation could reduce demand for transmission and thereby increase margins on transmission lines. Ultimately, a power system based on a large number of reliable small generators can operate with the same reliability and a lower capacity margin than a system with equally reliable large generators[70].

The main potential negative effect of distributed generation is an increased need for regulating (backup) power. This additional backup capacity will be needed if the DG technologies cannot be centrally controlled because of natural variability (wind and PV) or because of

---

70. Hoff, T., H. Wenger, C. Herig and R. Shaw, 1997.

operating characteristics (e.g. CHP where power output is matched to heat demand). Power systems with a larger share of these resources tend to increase transmission requirements, if reserve power is most economically available through interconnection with neighbouring systems.

The Danish transmission and distribution network illustrates both effects. The implementation of policies to favour wind power and CHP in the Danish system has reportedly led to a increased investment in the lower voltages (10 kV and 60 kV) but reduced loading on the 132 kV and 150 kV systems. However, the high-voltage system (400 kV) is being expanded in part to meet increased load and partly because of the need for greater regulating power that CHP and wind are unable to provide[71]. Interconnection with neighbouring countries in Nordel eases the problem because it provides access to power generation that can respond in real time. Nevertheless, a Nordel report has identified the expansion of wind and CHP as a design concern that it is studying[72]. The report notes that a big expansion optimally will require more than one network regulator to achieve balancing regulation throughout the system, given existing flow constraints. The report suggests that "distributed network regulation", where subareas of Nordel each have their own regulator, may be needed[73].

Summary

How does distribution generation measure up against the three Es of economic efficiency, energy security, and environment? It is difficult to generalise when discussing such a wide range of technologies with a wide range of characteristics. Regarding economic efficiency, the decision to build distributed generation is largely an issue for an individual customer. The policy issue is principally to ensure that the customer has access to markets – through retail liberalisation – and suitable price signals – from grid pricing. As for energy security, there

---

71. See CIGRE, 1999.
72. See Nordel 2000.
73. Increased use of large energy-storage technologies (such as compressed air storage or large regenerative fuel cells known as "flow batteries") may be part of the solution to this problem.

is a small concern about the increased use of gas (or fuel oil) in power generation. This issue is offset, however, by the enlarged generation capacity of systems with a larger share of DG. Regarding the environment, while distributed generation as a whole does not have clear benefits compared with the best-performing new plants, unless it uses CHP, it may do so compared with the existing mix of generating capacity. Environmental policies related to DG need to keep both of these aspects in mind.

FUTURE OF DISTRIBUTED GENERATION IN ELECTRICITY NETWORKS

Generation Technology Research and Development

The wide range of potential applications and favourable government policies for CHP and for renewables is likely to ensure a greater market share for distributed generation over the next decade. One estimate suggests that distributed generation worldwide could account for 7%-14% of total additions to generating capacity through increased use in, e.g. industrial cogeneration, microgeneration, and decentralised peaking units.

For DG to grow by this amount, the cost of technology has to decline. Substantial private and some government efforts aim at reducing the costs of a variety of DG technologies, particular fuel cells and photovoltaic systems. Improvements to fuel efficiency and declines in the capital cost of microturbines are needed to greatly enlarge their market, since natural gas prices are expected to rise in the future. Research continues on improving the efficiency of engines.

The more established technologies, engines and gas turbines, also may to be developed further to enhance environmental performance, given the trend toward tighter NO_x emissions standards. Research and development may need to focus on low-cost NO_x controls.

As for CHP development, there are two promising areas for further R&D:

■ **Less expensive, smaller absorption-cooling equipment.** The market for cooling and power generation in commercial buildings is potentially large. To date, the higher capital cost and larger size of absorption-cooling equipment has limited its penetration.

■ **Adjustable power CHP.** Market liberalisation is putting a greater premium on generating output that can respond to changing system conditions. CHP whose power can be adjusted could be a profitable technology as retail electricity markets develop.

The increased demand for uninterrupted power supplies could make energy-storage technologies (such as flywheels) important complementary technologies.

Implications for Electricity Network Design

How might the electricity system evolve if distributed generation and distributed power play a larger role? For example, if micro-CHP technologies or fuel cells become successful, what changes to the local distribution network will be required? As mentioned in the introduction, increased distributed power may be the third generation of electricity reform. While the first generation created independent power producers that sell power to utilities and the second created wholesale and retail markets, the third generation may involve power generated directly at the sites of customers.

The third generation may evolve in three distinct stages[74]:

■ **Accommodation.** Distributed generation is accommodated into the current market with the right price signals. Centralised control of the networks remains in place.

■ **Decentralisation.** The share of DG increases. Virtual utilities optimise the services of decentralised providers through the use of common communications systems[75]. Monitoring and control by local utilities is still required.

■ **Dispersal.** Distributed power takes over the electricity market. Microgrids and power parks effectively meet their own supply with limited recourse to grid-based electricity[76]. Distribution operates more like a co-ordinating agent between separate systems rather than controller of the system.

---

74. *See, for example, Lougheed, J. 2001.*
75. *See, for example, Bitsch, R. 2000.*
76. *See Hoff T., H. Wenger, C. Herig, and R. Shaw, 1997.*

This report is concerned mainly with the first of these three stages: how to accommodate distributed generation in the existing liberalised energy market. However, if the cost of generating capacity falls sharply as a result of greater use of DG, the market may move towards decentralisation and even dispersal.

There are already some signs of decentralisation. Technology is already being used to run emergency generators at customer sites. This technology enables a company, acting like a virtual utility[77], to control both individual customer loads and generation at several sites simultaneously through the Internet. Distribution planning studies are beginning to take distributed generation into account[78].

The integration of large numbers of distributed generators supplying power directly into distribution networks is more challenging and requires additional research. The operation and control of a distribution network of this type is different than that of a network with a few generators. The distribution network operator of the future will need the ability to:

■ optimise the operation of the system to supply power and ancillary services, and to minimise losses; and

■ protect the system against faults in the individual generators.

The system operator will need to do so for complex systems, which may comprise very flexible elements that can be co-ordinated and controlled locally. These elements may include wind power and PV systems, both of which are highly variable, and increased use of CHP, whose electric output varies with heat demand[79].

Even if networks are managed in a decentralised way, for example, with individual customers responding to the needs of the local network, they will require a greatly increased flow of information to ensure smooth operation of the system. The distribution utility of the future will need to be in a position to provide information, and to monitor and control its own system in a more sophisticated manner. The first step is development of hardware and software for the more

---

77. *See, for example, Cohen, D. 2001.*
78. *See Peco J. and T. Gomez, 2000.*
79. *Handschein, E. 2001.*

sophisticated monitoring and operational control over the distribution system. This would include increased control and co-ordination of DG operations through the distribution system, associated communications devices, more elaborate protection systems to account for the presence of distributed generation, and more sophisticated metering. As distributed generation increases its share of total power generation, the design specifications of distribution systems will need to evolve, just as the capabilities of other network industries such as telecommunications have had to develop. Research efforts such as the Dispower project for the European Commission is addressing these issues[80].

Therefore, a much more sophisticated institution will be needed in the future to manage the distribution of electricity. Distribution companies have already drastically evolved from simply providing electricity at a regulated price to supplying "distribution network services" to electricity consumers. However, the change to a company that is capable of actively managing a large number of generators on their network is even larger step.

The emergence of decentralised systems also requires energy-service providers acting as virtual utilities. In principle, these entities may simply operate and manage a co-ordination service of distributed energy resources owned by several customers. They are also potentially vehicles for building, owning, and operating generating assets at customer sites. The build-own-operate model has been successfully in the development of distributed generation in Japan. It has the advantage of allowing the customer to avoid the complexities and the financial risks involved in developing their own power-generation assets. Thus, the "virtual utility" becomes in many respects a "real" entity that uses its superior financing capability to develop the distributed resource market more rapidly than otherwise would be the case.

---

80. *EC Research, 2001.*

CONCLUSIONS AND RECOMMENDATIONS

Distributed generation already represents a small but important share of power generation in the OECD. Diesel engines make up much of the installed generating capacity of distributed generation but little of its power generation. Combined heat and power technologies already make a substantial contribution to total power production in several OECD countries. A small number of remote OECD electricity consumers are supplied by decentralised grids. Worldwide demand for distributed power generation capacity in 2000 was 7% of total orders, which is small but greater than new construction of nuclear generating capacity.

Distributed generation is expected to play a greater role in OECD power generation over the next decade. There is a growing interest by power consumers to install their own generating capacity to:

■ Take advantage of the flexibility of DG technologies to produce power during favourable times and to expand output readily in response to increased requirements.

■ Use existing emergency or standby generators to supply power during peak periods.

■ Supply heating and cooling needs, and sell electricity.

■ Improve the reliability and quality of power consumed.

Concerns about reliability can drive the purchase of DG capacity, if network reliability is insufficient for a customer's needs. While this kind of capacity contributes little to overall electricity production, it is expected to become an increasingly important source of peak supply. In this way, distributed generation will contribute to the security of electricity supply. However, the introduction of increased wind and CHP systems may increase the need for reserve capacity.

Combining heating, cooling, and power generation is proving to be an important niche for distributed power, aided in some countries by favourable policies. As long as effective use of heat generation is ensured, CHP also has the advantage of reducing greenhouse-gas emissions, compared with conventional fossil power and heat generation. Much of the growth of CHP will be driven by favourable government policies. Additional research and development work is required to improve environmental performance and reduce the costs of some technologies.

There are hundreds of thousands of electricity customers in the OECD in remote communities served by distributed generation. These consumers cannot enjoy the benefits of electricity-market liberalisation. One option to increase competition and thus reduce energy costs in these communities is to encourage these consumers, through pricing policies that include the full cost of generation, to generate their own electricity and supply their local community.

Retail market liberalisation will play the key role in opening up economically efficient development of distributed generation in the longer term, by giving consumers access to the distribution system. Structural reform will leave the distributor indifferent rather than in competition with distributed generation. Unbundled pricing will make it possible, at least in principle, for a distributed generator to capture the value it brings to a distribution system and to pay the costs it imposes.

Conversely, distributed generation promotes retail market liberalisation by giving power consumers additional options for power supply and creating more competitive power producers.

So far, the opening of electricity markets has hurt distributed producers in some markets. Some problems are related to increased transactions costs, which affect smaller producers more than larger producers. However, the main problem has been an increase in natural gas prices and a fall in electricity prices. Some governments have established programmes to support CHP producers that were affected by liberalisation.

Many institutional and regulatory barriers continue to thwart the full development of distributed generation:

■ In many OECD jurisdictions, partially liberalised markets leave distributed generation, due to a lack of legal access to the distribution grid, in competition with the utility.

■ The lack of standards for connection of smaller distributed generation increases transaction costs for distributor and distributed generator.

■ The variation in capabilities of distribution companies.

■ The lack of incentives for distribution companies to encourage DG and power exports to the grid that reduce system costs.

■ Emissions regulations that are overly demanding for small sources.

Reforms to OECD electricity markets, therefore, need to ensure that distributed generators can obtain access to local electricity grids and do not compete with the distribution company for supply. Regulators will play a key role in ensuring that distributors, instead of discriminating against distributed generators, are rewarded when they encourage distributed generation that reduces distribution network costs. Standardising interconnection rules would reduce transaction costs.

The benefits of distributed generation to grids are specific to location and difficult to quantify. While location-based pricing is increasingly used for central generation, it is not yet practised for distributed generation. If distributed generators are to be encouraged to locate suitably, distributors will need to make information available on more suitable locations. Distributors in turn will need regulatory encouragement to improve their performance at least cost, and so be rewarded when additional distributed generation reduces system costs.

When compared with the existing mix of generating capacity in most OECD countries, both renewable and CHP distributed-generation technologies offer environmental advantages. However, fossil-fired distributed technologies not using CHP, or even those using CHP and not using natural gas as fuel, will generally have higher specific emissions of both greenhouse gases and nitrogen oxides compared with large combined-cyle gas generation technologies. Environmental regulations need to take into account that small is not necessarily beautiful, and accommodate more efficient technologies such as CHP. Standards are very useful in encouraging the uptake of more efficient CHP technology. Economic instruments such as taxes or emissions permits can give all generating technologies incentives to reduce emissions. Internalising the external cost of pollution (e.g. through taxation) also will result in a more optimal mix of electricity production.

In developing policies to promote some distributed technologies, there is a temptation to modify the design or operation of the electricity market. The difficulty with such approaches is that they reduce economic efficiency in the operation of the power system and thus incur costs that might otherwise have been avoided. Given that distributed generation comprises heterogeneous technologies, changing electricity market rules for them on environmental grounds alone is inappropriate. However, other mechanisms can and have been implemented to further raise the share of "environmentally benign" distributed-generation technologies in total power generation.

It is difficult to estimate the current level of DG capacity in OECD electricity markets because of a lack of national statistics. Distributed generation tends to be invisible to policy makers except where it is being supported for other purposes, e.g. the environment. Good data about distribution generation will become necessary as it begins to play an important role in electricity markets.

Over the long haul, changes are needed to the design of distribution systems to accommodate distributed generation. Simply put, distribution companies need to become more sophisticated. Distribution systems must be capable of accommodating two-way flow, and have greater communications and control capabilities. The skills required to operate and manage a distribution system will become correspondingly more complex. Such technical and institutional changes technically would make feasible a more decentralised electric power system.

Recommendations

■ Market Access

■ Liberalise electricity markets to ensure access to the distribution system by distributed generators.

■ Separate distribution network operations from the competitive business of retail supply.

■ Standardise interconnection rules for distributed generation.

■ Market Organisation

■ Where feasible, establish wholesale-market trading arrangements that allow distributed power to participate in the provision of energy, reserve, or ancillary services.

■ Ensure that wholesale-market trading arrangements have effective mechanisms that can help smaller generators participate in these markets.

■ Consider developing the technical capabilities of distribution networks to accommodate greater proportions of distributed generation.

■ Pricing

■ Consider location-based pricing for transmission to give incentives to generators, including distributed generators, to locate closer to loads.

■ Consider location-based pricing for distribution that:

• provides incentives to distributors to connect distributed generation when it reduces overall distribution costs;

• rewards distributed generation where it can help relieve transmission or distribution congestion, reduce losses, or provide system services; and

• avoids using grid pricing as a way to subsidise distributed generation.

■ Recover grid reinforcement costs for distributed generation through use of system charges rather than connection fees.

■ Ensure that prices for services such as balancing reflect costs for all generators.

■ Consider pricing electricity for remote consumers that includes the full cost of generation, to encourage efficiency and the development of self-generation.

■ Environment

■ Consider both size, and short-term and long-term impacts when regulating air emissions from distributed generation.

■ Consider including distributed generators in policies and measures to reduce greenhouse-gas emissions, to encourage them to improve their fuel efficiency or use renewable fuels.

■ Develop policies to encourage consumers in off-grid systems to develop their own power generation.

■ Consider that policies that promote the use of CHP are likely to improve efficiency and reduce emissions.

■ Energy Security

■ Develop policies, which include emissions limits, to ensure that standby-power generators can access markets.

■ Research and Development

■ Focus distributed generation R&D on:

• Decreasing costs and reduced emissions from generation.

• Increasing the flexibility of electric output from the operation of CHP plants.

• Evaluating the impact of increased DG on design requirements for distribution systems.

■ Other

- ■ Develop and collect statistics on distributed generation.

ANNEX I

Comparing Energy Consumption and Emissions from On-site CHP and Conventional Heat and Power Generation

■ Introduction

Several IEA countries have specific policies to promote combined heat and power (CHP) generation as a way to save energy and to reduce emissions, particularly of carbon dioxide. One question that inevitably arises is: how much are fuel consumption and emissions reduced compared with heat supply by conventional boilers and electricity supply from grid-based electricity.

The answer to this question involves making assumptions about the technologies displaced by the CHP plant. The choice of technologies may well be guided by consideration of short-term versus long-term perspectives. For example, it would be reasonable to assume that, in the short term, a CHP plant would replace boilers that are currently located at the site (but remain available for backup purposes) as well as the current average grid electricity. A longer-term perspective might assume that a general policy to promote CHP plant would displace new conventional generation (e.g. combined-cycle gas turbines) and new boilers.

This annex presents simple formulae for comparing fuel consumption, and CO_2 and NO_x emissions from on-site CHP facilities with power supply from the grid and heat production from a boiler. Two examples using data from other research (DTI, 2000 and Kaarsberg et al., 1998) illustrate the use of the formulae. A third example, examining diesel-fired CHP in India, shows large potential for CHP savings in power systems in developing countries. Finally, there is a brief discussion of different methods of allocating emissions between power and heat.

■ Comparing Fuel Consumption and Emissions

a) Comparison of fuel consumption

The fuel input, and heat and power outputs for a CHP plant versus that of a boiler and grid electricity can be visualised as follows:

i) CHP plant input and output

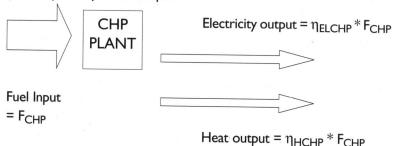

Electricity output = $\eta_{ELCHP} * F_{CHP}$

Fuel Input
= F_{CHP}

Heat output = $\eta_{HCHP} * F_{CHP}$

ii) Electricity system and on-site boiler input and output

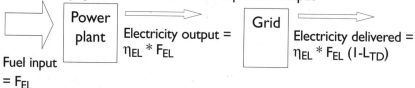

Power plant — Electricity output = $\eta_{EL} * F_{EL}$

Grid — Electricity delivered = $\eta_{EL} * F_{EL} (1-L_{TD})$

Fuel input
= F_{EL}

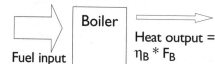

Boiler — Heat output = $\eta_B * F_B$

Fuel input
= F_B

where:

F_{CHP} = fuel input to CHP plant

F_B = fuel input to boiler

F_{EL} = fuel input to power generation

η_{ELCHP} = net electrical efficiency of CHP plant

η_{HCHP} = heat efficiency of CHP plant

η_B = heat efficiency of boiler

η_{EL} = net electrical efficiency of electricity generator

L_{TD} = transmission and distribution losses of grid electricity

To produce the same quantity of electricity and heat, the delivered electricity from the grid must equal the electricity produced by the CHP plant and the heat produced by the boiler must equal the heat produced by the CHP plant, i.e. :

$$\eta_{EL} * F_{EL} (1-L_{TD}) = \eta_{ELCHP} * F_{CHP}$$

and

$$\eta_B * F_B = \eta_{HCHP} * F_{CHP}$$

Then the ratio of fuel consumed by separate heat and electricity generation versus CHP is given by :

$$\frac{\text{Fuel consumed by grid power and boiler } (F_{EL} + F_B)}{\text{Fuel consumed by CHP } (F_{CHP})}$$

$$= \frac{\eta_{ELCHP}}{\eta_{EL} * (1-L_{TD})} + \frac{\eta_{HCHP}}{\eta_B}$$

> 1 for the CHP to save energy compared with separate systems

b) Comparison of emissions

Calculating the emissions of NO_x or CO_2 from the CHP plant is relatively straightforward.

Emissions for the ith pollutant (e.g. NO_x or CO_2) from CHP
= $EF_{iCHP} * F_{CHP}(GJ)$

Where EF_{iCHP} is the emissions of a particular pollutant per unit of fuel input to the CHP plant (g/GJ).

Comparing emissions is somewhat more complicated since different fuels and emissions control technologies (for NO_x) can result in large changes in the emissions factors and hence the results. Nevertheless, one can calculate the ratio:

$$\frac{\text{Emissions}_i \text{ (separate)}}{\text{Emissions}_i \text{ (CHP)}} = \frac{EF_{iEL} * \eta_{ELCHP}}{EF_{iCHP} * \eta_{EL} * (1-L_{TD})} + \frac{EF_{iB} * \eta_{HCHP}}{EF_{iCHP} * \eta_B}$$

$$> 1$$

for the CHP to save emissions compared with separate systems

Note that for CO_2 emissions, if the input fuels are the same for CHP plant, boiler and grid electricity, the ratio of emissions equals the ratio of fuel consumption. However, for NO_x emissions, even when the same fuel is used for all three processes, emission factors are different because of different NO_x control technologies.

■ Examples

CO_2 Emissions from CHP Compared with Displaced Grid Electricity and Boiler Emissions in the UK

The UK Department of Trade and Industry has analysed the carbon-dioxide emissions from UK CHP plants and compared them with the average UK fossil grid and UK boiler emissions displaced (see DTI, 2000). The DTI analysis assumes that only emissions from fossil-fired power stations are displaced at the current mix. They estimate that the fossil mix (including coal, gas and oil) has an average efficiency (accounting for losses) of 38.7% with average CO_2 emissions per unit of electricity output (= $EF_{CEL}/\eta_{EL} * (1-L_{TD})$) of 183 gC/kWh. The boiler mix (which includes oil and coal as well as gas boilers) has an average efficiency of 75% with average emissions per unit heat output (= EF_{CB}/η_B) of 81 gC/kWh. The average emission factor for CHP is 43.3 gC/kWh. This is a relatively low value as approximately one-quarter of CHP production in the UK is from waste or renewable fuels, which are considered to have zero greenhouse-gas emissions. The electric efficiency is 18.4% and heat efficiency is 49.2%. Relative energy consumption is:

$$\frac{\text{Fuel consumed (separate)}}{\text{Fuel consumed (CHP)}} = 18.4\%/37.7\% + 49.2\%/75\% = 1.13$$

In other words, energy consumption is 13% higher when the power and heat are generated separately than by CHP, implying fuel savings of approximately 11% when CHP is used.

For carbon emissions:

$$\frac{\text{Emissions (separate)}}{\text{Emissions (CHP)}} = 183 * 0.184/43.3 + 81*0.492/43.3 = 1.7$$

implying that emissions from the ensemble of CHP facilities are 41% lower.

NO$_x$ Emissions from an Efficient Gas Engine Versus US Average and New CCGT

Kaarsberg et al. 1998 estimate NO$_x$ emissions for a gas engine and compare them to the US grid average data. In their case, they assume that a gas engine generates electricity at 39% efficiency and has a heat efficiency of 50%. NO$_x$ emissions are 108 g/GJ of fuel input or 1.0 g/kWh of electricity output. In one example, they assume the engine replaces an average boiler (65% efficient, emissions of 120 g/GJ) and the US average grid (30% efficient, with 2.18 g NO$_x$/kWh delivered electricity). This gives the ratio of emissions:

$= 2.18/1.00 + 0.50*120/108*0.65 = 2.54$

implying a 60% emissions reduction by using CHP.

However, a second example assumes a new gas boiler (85% efficient, with NO$_x$ emissions at 24 g/GJ i.e. 80% lower) and a new combined-cycle gas turbine 55% efficient, with NO$_x$ emissions of 0.05 g/kWh (or over 40 times lower than the grid average):

$= 0.05/1.00 +0.50*24/108*0.85 = 0.14$

implying that NO$_x$ emissions from reciprocating engine CHP are seven times **higher** than used for separate new technologies.

Diesel CHP in India

In developed countries, the relatively high efficiencies of both power plants and grids reduces the emissions impact of central generation. However, central power systems in developing countries may have poorer technical performance. One example is India, where the power system is heavily reliant on coal, much of it of low quality, and transmission and distribution losses are very high, averaging 22% including "nontechnical" losses (technical losses alone have been estimated at 13%), compared with an OECD average of 6.8%. Power reliability problems make distributed power an attractive option for some Indian industries. Industrial power-generating capacity amounts to 15 GW, of which 6 GW is by diesel generation.

As a consequence, an efficient industrial-size diesel generation CHP unit can have a significant carbon-emissions benefit compared with grid electricity. In 1999, the Indian electric utility power system produced 478 TWh of electricity from 4840 PJ of fuel and emitted 399 Mt of CO_2 (given an average efficiency of 35.5% and 82.4 kg CO_2/GJ of fuel input). A 43% efficient diesel engine has an emissions factor of 74.1 kg CO_2/GJ of fuel used. Assuming that the CHP produces heat at 37% efficiency and that it replaces an oil boiler at 75% efficiency (carbon emissions factor of 74.1 kgCO_2/GJ), the emissions ratio is :

$$= 82.4*(0.43)/(74.1*0.355*0.87) + 74.1*0.37/(74.1*0.75) = 2.04$$

Thus, replacing grid electricity with diesel-fired CHP reduces emissions by 51%, even allowing for non-fossil production for the grid. If it is assumed that the diesel generator replaces coal-fired generation only (which averages 32% efficiency and has a higher carbon-emissions factor), emissions with diesel CHP are 60% lower than from grid electricity and separate oil boiler.

Quality Index for UK "Good Quality CHP"

The above analysis shows that develop a definition of CHP that saves energy and emissions is straightforward. For governments developing fiscal or other policies to favour CHP, energy and emissions-saving criteria can easily be used to screen eligibility. The UK government has used such an approach in developing a Quality Index for CHP schemes that want to qualify for a variety of fiscal benefits.

The Quality Index is defined as (DETR, 2001).

Quality Index (QI) = $X\eta_{ELCHP} + Y \eta_{HCHP}$.

Where X and Y are parameters that vary with the size of the CHP project (for a 10-25 MW project X = 205, Y = 125).

The requirements for good quality CHP include :

$\eta_{ELCHP} > 0.2$

and QI > 100.

Comparing the result with the first equation on energy savings

$$X = 1/\eta_{EL} * (1-L_{TD}) \qquad \text{for } X = 205$$
$$\eta_{EL} * (1-L_{TD}) = 100/205 = 0.488$$

$$Y = 1/\eta_B \quad \text{for } Y = 125 \quad \eta_B = 0.8.$$

Given that the current electricity system and boilers in the UK have much lower average efficiency than CHP, the Quality Index criterion implies that a CHP project must result in a large energy savings to qualify as "Good Quality CHP". This is illustrated in the figure below.

Figure A1

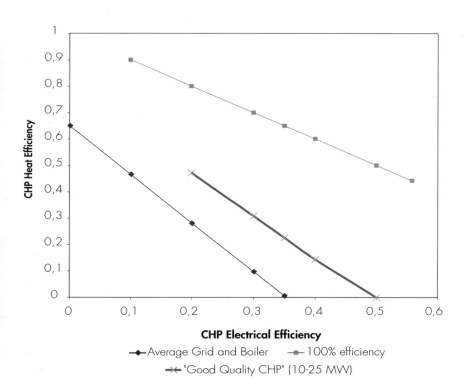

Comparison of Good Quality CHP Output with Average UK Grid

CHP Heat Efficiency (y-axis)

CHP Electrical Efficiency (x-axis)

→ Average Grid and Boiler ─■─ 100% efficiency
→← "Good Quality CHP" (10-25 MW)

Allocating CHP Emissions to Electricity Production and Heat Production[81]

While the above analyses calculate the overall emissions benefit of CHP, it may be necessary to allocate emissions to power generation or heat separately. One reason is statistical: emissions from power production and from heat production are often recorded separately[82]. Also, some emissions regulations or trading schemes (for carbon dioxide and for NO_x) focus exclusively on the power-generation sector. Third, customers for the heat and for the electricity may be different and thus need to be charged separately.

The actual allocation is notional. There are three different methods:

■ **Allocate remaining emissions to power generation.** Emissions from heat are assumed equal to some comparator e.g. a boiler with a given fuel and efficiency. Emissions remaining are allocated to power generation. This approach would allocate all emissions savings to power generation. This convention is used by the European Community.

■ **Allocate remaining emissions to heat.** Emissions from electricity production are assumed equal to some comparator, i.e. grid electricity. Remaining emissions are then allocated to heat production. This approach allocates all emissions savings to heat production.

■ **Split the allocation.** This approach recognises that more fuel is required to make electricity than heat, and allocates fuel use and emissions to the two outputs likewise. The UK guidelines for company reporting on greenhouse-gas emissions allocates twice as much fuel (and associated emissions) per unit of power generated from a CHP project as per unit of heat generated.

---

81. *This discussion is largely derived from DTI, 2000.*
82. *IEA statistics record these emissions jointly and estimate emissions rates (in gCO_2/kWh) by adding the heat output to the electrical output.*

BIBLIOGRAPHY

Alderfer, B., M. Eldridge, and T. Starrs, 2000. *Making Connections : Case Studies of Interconnection Barriers and their Impacts on Distributed Power Projects*, National Renewable Energy Laboratory, Golden, Colorado.

Bitsch, R., 2000. "Decentralised Energy Supply Options in Industrialised & Developing Countries", *WorldPower 2000*, Siemens AG, 61-65.

CARB, 2001. "Guideline for the Permitting of Electrical Generation Technologies", State of California Environmental Protection Agency, Air Resources Board, Stationary Source Division, September 2001.

Caudron, L., 2000. "Distributed Energy : Fad or Inevitable Evolution ? Summary and Closing Remarks", *Decentralised Power 2000*, Nice, France, 7-9 February 2000.

CEC, 2000. *The Role of Energy Efficiency and Distributed Generation in Grid Planning*, California Energy Commission, Report to the Governor and Legislature, Publication # 300-00-003, April 2000.

CEC, 2001. "BUGS-1, Database of Public Back-up Generators in California", California Energy Commission, 15 August 2001.

CIGRE, 1999. *Impact of Increasing Contribution of Dispersed Generation on the Power System*, CIGRÉ (Conseil International des Grands Réseaux Électriques) Working Group Report 137, February 1999.

CIRED, 1999. *CIRED Working group No. 4 on Dispersed Generation, Preliminary Report For Discussion at CIRED 1999*, Congrès International des Réseaux Electriques de Distribution, 1999.

Chapel S. and C. Feinstein, 2000. "Strategic Role of DR in Distribution Systems", *EPRI Workshop on Distributed Resource Economic Evaluation*, Chicago, 13 December 2000.

CHPQA, 2000. "Defining Good Quality CHP", Guidance Note 10, CHPQA, UK Department of Environment, Food and Rural Affairs, 2000.

CGC Japan, 2001. *Current State and Trend of Cogeneration in Japan*, CGC Japan Cogeneration Center, January 2001.

Cogen Europe, 1999. *The Administrative Obstacles to the Development of Decentralised Cogeneration – Electrical Network Limits*, Cogen Europe, 1999.

Cogen Europe, 2000. Press Release, "Electricity Liberalisation : A Disaster for Clean Energy", Brussels, 7 March 2000.

Cohen, D. 2001. "Using Real-Time Web Technology to Manage DE Networks", Silicon Energy, *Distributed Power 2001*, Intertech, Nice, France, May 2001.

Cotard, E. 2000. "Electricity Transport Regimes : Their Impact on Cogeneration", *Cogeneration and On-site Power Production*, No. 6, November-December 2000, 57-67.

Courcelle, B. 2001. "Distributed Generation : From a Global Market to Niche Applications", Honeywell, *Distributed Power 2001*, Nice, France, May 2001.

DTI EGWG, 2001. Embedded Generation Working Group, *Report into Network Issues for Embedded Generation*, Volume 1 Main Report and Volume 2, Annexes, UK Department of Trade and Industry, January 2001.

DTI, 2000. *Savings in Carbon Emissions from Combined Heat and Power*, Energy Trends, October 2000.

DTI, 2001a. *Digest of United Kingdom Energy Statistics 2001*, UK Department of Trade and Industry, July 2001.

DTI, 2001b. "Wilson Seeks System Changes for Green Generators", DTI Press Release, 30 November 2001.

DTI, 2001c. *Government Response to Ofgem's Reports "The New Electricity Trading Arrangements – Review of the First Three Months" and "Report to the DTI on the Review of the Initial Impact of NETA on Small Generators" of 31 August 2001*, UK Department of Trade and Industry, 1 November 2001.

DGTW, 2001. "Orders up Across all Engine Ranges" (24th Annual Power Generation Survey), *Diesel and Gas Turbine Worldwide* (www.dieselpub.com/ww/ww_power2000.htm).

DTE, 2001. "DTe : Increase in Market Forces through the Relaxation of the Imbalance System", DTE (Office for Energy Regulation) Press Release, 5 March 2001.

Dunn, S. 2000. *Micropower: The Next Electrical Era*, Worldwatch Institute, Washington, DC, Paper 151, July 2000.

EC, 1997. "A Community Strategy to Promote Combined Heat and Power (CHP) and to Dismantle Barriers to its Development", European Commission, COM (97) 514, 15 October 1997.

EC Research, 2001. "Distributed Generation with High Penetration of Renewable Sources – DISPOWER", EC Research, ftp ://ftp.cordis.lu/pub/eesd/docs/ev260901_poster_dispower.pdf, 20 September 2001.

ECN, 2000. *Energy Market Trends in the Netherlands 2000,* ECN (The Netherlands Energy Research Foundation), 2000.

EIA, 2000. *Annual Energy Outlook 2001*, Energy Information Administration, US Department of Energy, Report# :DOE/EIA-0383(2001), December 2000.

EIA, 2001. *Modeling Distributed Electricity Generation in the NEMS Buildings Models*, Erin Boedecker, John Cymbalsky and Stephen Wade, Energy Information Administration, US Department of Energy, www.eia.doe.ogv/oiaf/analysispaper/electricity_generation.html, last modified 28 August 2001.

Frayer, J. and N. Uludere,2001. "What is it Worth ? Application of Real Options Theory to the Valuation of Generation Assets", *Electricity Journal,* Volume 13, Issue 8, 40-51.

Future Cogen, 2001. *The Future of CHP in the European Market – The European Cogeneration Study*, prepared for the European Commission SAVE program, Report no. XVII/4.1031/P/99-169, May 2001.

 BIBLIOGRAPHY

Gas Research Institute, 1999. *The Role of Distributed Generation in Competitive Energy Markets.*

Gillette, S. 2001. "Emerging Technology Markets : Microturbines", *2nd International CHP Symposium,* Amsterdam, the Netherlands, May 2001.

Handschein, E. 2001. Integration, Control and Management of Dispersed Generation, *Distributed Power 2001,* Intertech, Nice, France, May 2001.

Hangai, E. 2001. "MyEnergy's On-site Energy Service based on Customer Perspective", MyEnergy presentation, 4 April 2001.

T. Hoff, H. Wenger, C. Herig, and R. Shaw, Jr., 1997. "Distributed Generation and Microgrids", *18th USAEE/IAEE*, San Francisco, California, September 1997, available at http ://www.clean-power.com/research/microgrids/MicroGrids.pdf.

Huhn, K., 2001. "Cogeneration in Europe Heading for Applications below 10 kW", *Cogeneration and On-Site Power Production*, July-August 2001, 55-59.

IEA, 2000. *Energy Policies of the Netherlands, 2000 Review,* International Energy Agency, Paris, 2000.

IEA, 2001a. *Energy Prices and Taxes,* 3rd Quarter 2001, Paris, 2001.

IEA 2001b. *WEO Insights 2001 : Today's Energy Supplies Fuelling Tomorrow's Growth,* International Energy Agency, Paris, 2001.

IEA 2002. *Security of Supply in Electricity Markets : Evidence and Policy Issues,* International Energy Agency, Paris, 2002.

IEA Wind 2001, *IEA Wind Energy Annual Report 2000*, International Energy Agency Implementing Agreement for Co-operation in the Research and Development of Wind Turbine Systems, May 2001.

Kaarsberg, T., J. Bluestein, J. Romm, and A. Rosenfeld, 1998. "The Outlook for Small Scale CHP in the USA", CADDET Energy Efficiency Newsletter No. 2, 1998.

Kirby, B. and E. Hirst 2001. Kirby, *Bulk-Power Reliability and Commercial Implications of Distributed Resources*, NARUC, April 2000, (http ://www.ornl.gov/ORNL/BTC/Restructuring/Rapdr.pdf).

Jenkins, N., R. Allan, P. Crossley D. Kirschen, and G. Strbac, 2000. *Embedded Generation*, The Institution of Electrical Engineers, London, 2000.

Arthur D. Little, Inc., *Distributed Generation : Policy Framework for Regulators*, Cambridge, Massachusetts, 1999.

Arthur D. Little, Inc., *Distributed Generation : System Interfaces*, Cambridge, Massachusetts, 1999.

Arthur D. Little, Inc., *Distributed Generation : Understanding the Economics*, Cambridge, Massachusetts, 1999.

Lenssen, N., "Current and Future Markets for Distributed Generation in the OECD", presentation to *Aspen Clean Energy Roundtable VII*, 27-29 September 2000.

Lönnroth, M., 1989. "The Coming Reformation of the Electric Utility Industry", *Electricity, Efficient End Use and New Generation Technologies, and Their Planning Implications*, T.B. Johannson editor, 1989, 765-786.

METI, 2001. *Preliminary Report on the 1999 Structural Survey of Energy Consumption*, Japan Ministry of Economy, Trade and Industry, 2001.

Milford, L. 2001. "The Harvard Medical School Fuel Cell Project", Clean Energy Group, 2nd International CHP Symposium, Amsterdam, the Netherlands, May 2001.

NEA/IEA, 1998. *Projected Costs of Generating Electricity Update 1998*, Nuclear Energy Agency and International Energy Agency, Paris 1998.

NEGA, 2001. "Survey on Installation of Non-emergency On-site Power Generation Facilities", Japan Engine Generator Association, annual surveys 1997-2000 (in Japanese).

 BIBLIOGRAPHY

Nordel, 2000. *Non-dispatchable Production in the Nordel System*, Nordel's Grid Group, May 2000.

NYISO, 2001. NY Independent System Operation, *Emergency Demand Response Program Status Report*, 20 August 2001.

Onsite Sycom Energy Corporation 2000a. *Interconnection in California : Connecting Distributed Generation to the Grid*, Consultant's Report to the California Energy Commission, October 2000.

Onsite Sycom Energy Corporation 2000b. *The Market and Technical Potential for Combined Heat and Power in the Commercial/Institutional Sector*, prepared for the US Department of Energy, Energy Information Administration, January 2000 (revision 1).

Onsite Sycom Energy Corporation 2000c. *The Market and Technical Potential for Combined Heat and Power in the Industrial Sector*, prepared for the US Department of Energy, Energy Information Administration, January 2000.

Ofgem 2001a. *Report to the DTI on the Review of the Initial Impact of NETA on Smaller Generators*, UK Office of Gas and Electricity Markets, August 2001.

Ofgem 2001b. *Embedded Generation : Price Controls, Incentives and Connection Charging, a Preliminary Consultation Document*, UK Office of Gas and Electricity Markets, September 2001.

Pati, M., Ristau, R., Sheblé, G., and M. Wilhelm 2001. *Real Option Valuation of Distributed Generation Interconnection*, prepared for the Edison Electric Institute, March 2001.

Patterson, W. 1999. Royal Institute of International Affairs, *Transforming Electricity : The Coming Generation of Change*, Earthscan, London, 1999.

Peco, J. and T. Gomez, 2000. "A Model for Planning Large Scale MV Networks considering Uncertainty in Reliability Modelling", 6th International Conference on Probabilistic Methods Applied to Power Systems, Funchal, Madeira -Portugal, 25-28 September 2000.

Peltier, R. 2001. "Proven Performers Capture DG market", *Power*, July/August 2001, 44-50.

Perrault, L., 2001. "CHP and the Information Age – Cooling and Ultra-reliable Power for Data Centres", *Cogeneration and On-Site Power Production*, July-August 2001, 61-63.

Primen, 2001. *The Cost of Power Disturbances to Industrial and Digital Economy Companies*, by Primen Consultants, submitted to EPRI's Consortium for Electric Infrastructure for a Digital Society, June 2001.

RAP, 2001. *Expected Emissions Output from Various Distributed Generation Technologies*, Regulatory Assistance Project, May 2001 (www.rapmaine.org).

SAVE, 2001. *Risks and Chances for Small Scale Combined Heat and Power in the Liberalised Energy Market, Final Report*, prepared by Ambiente Italia srl, Kraftwärmeanlagen GmbH, Eicher + Pauli AG, and CIT Energy Management AB, SAVE Contract XVII/4.1031/z/99-063, 30 March 2001.

Singh, V., 20001. *Blending Wind and Solar into the Diesel Generator Market*, Renewable Energy Policy Project Research Report No. 12, Winter 2001.

TNRCC, 2001. Texas Natural Resource Conservation Commission, *Air Quality Standard Permit for Electric Generating Units*, June 2001.

USDOE, 2000. *Strategic Plan for Distributed Energy Resources*, US Department of Energy, September 2000.

Zacharias, P and K. Rohrig, 2001. "Integration of Wind and other RE Sources in Power Supply", *Distributed Power 2001*, Nice France, 16-18 May 2001.